A PAPAGO TRAVELER

VOLUME 13
Sun Tracks
An American Indian Literary Series

SERIES EDITOR
Larry Evers

EDITORIAL COMMITTEE
Vine Deloria, Jr.
N. Scott Momaday
Emory Sekaquaptewa
Leslie Marmon Silko
Ofelia Zepeda

James McCarthy in World War I Uniform
Photo by Dan Tortorell, 1982

A PAPAGO TRAVELER

The Memories of James McCarthy

James McCarthy
Edited by
John G. Westover

Sun Tracks
and
The University of Arizona Press
Tucson, Arizona

About the Author
JAMES MCCARTHY, a Papago Indian, was born in 1895 on the main Papago Reservation, near Tucson, Arizona. His experiences, as recorded
in this autobiography, have swept almost a century of reservation life,
soldiering, itinerant labor, faith healing, and family living.

About the Editor
JOHN G. WESTOVER, a military historian, became interested in recording
Mr. McCarthy's soldier stories. A warm friendship developed between
the two men and led to Westover's editing of McCarthy's memoirs, the
first autobiography of a Papago man ever published.

Sun Tracks is an American Indian literary series sponsored by the
American Indian Studies Program and the Department of English,
University of Arizona, Tucson, Arizona. All correspondence concern-
ing text should be sent to: *Sun Tracks*, Department of English, Modern
Languages Building # 67, University of Arizona, Tucson, Arizona 85721.
All orders should be sent to: The University of Arizona Press, 1615 E.
Speedway, Tucson, Arizona 85719. Volumes 1 – 5 of *Sun Tracks* are out
of print. They are available on microfiche from Clearwater Publishing
Company, Inc., 1995 Broadway, New York, New York 10023.

THE UNIVERSITY OF ARIZONA PRESS

Copyright © 1985
The Arizona Board of Regents
All Rights Reserved

This book was set in 10/12 Compugraphic Trump
Manufactured in the U.S.A.

Library of Congress Cataloging-in-Publication Data

McCarthy, James, 1895 –
   A Papago traveler.

   (Sun tracks ; 13)
   Includes index.
   1. McCarthy, James, 1895 –   . 2. Papago Indians—
Biography. I. Westover, John Glendower, 1917 –
II. Title.   III. Series.
PS501.S85   vol. 13   810'.8 s [973'.0497] [B]   85-14138
[E99.P25]
ISBN 0-8165-0933-6
ISBN 0-8165-0942-5 (pbk.)

To Emilia, My Mrs.
She Was a Good Woman

Contents

Foreword, by Larry Evers   ix
Introduction, by John G. Westover   xiii

The Early Years, 1895 – 1906   1
Indian School Days, 1906 – 1917   26
The Army Years, 1917 – 1922   68
Seeing the Country, 1922 – 1929   99
The Family Man, 1929 – 1944   146
Faith and Healing, 1944 – 1957   160
The Retirement Years, 1957 Onward   185

Index   195

ILLUSTRATIONS

James McCarthy in 1982   *Frontispiece*
Page of Handwritten Manuscript   xii
Map: James McCarthy's Homeland   3

Foreword

The narrative of this Papago traveler may be unsettling for those of us whose experience with American Indians has been primarily a literary one. Reading it will make us look in a new way at some of our favorite literary images of the American Indian. For those who think that an Indian can only be truly at home when he is living in a tribal community attuned to the natural world around him, here is an Indian who seems to be comfortable and "at home" with himself whether he is in England or China or a trailer park in California. For those who think of service in a white man's war as one of the most disorienting and dislocating experiences possible for an Indian, here is a man who fought in the First World War and was not ruined by the experience, who, indeed, rose to meet the challenges of each new experience. For those who look to Indians for mystic, tribal ways of healing, here is one who cures by the sign of Christian Science. For those who would have their Indians disinterested in contemporary American culture, here is an Indian who yearned to see "the country" because there was always something new and interesting to learn. And here is an Indian who, without the benefit of a high school or college education, wrote his story himself.

More than one hundred other Native Americans have recorded their lives as book-length autobiographies, but most of these are "as-told-to" narratives, in which a Native American talks about his or her life and a non-Indian collaborator writes it down. Among these are two told by Papagos: one by María Chona, who collaborated with Columbia University anthropologist Ruth Underhill between 1931 and 1933 to produce an account of Chona's life now available as *Papago Woman* (1936; rpt. New York: Holt, Rinehart, and Winston, 1979), and one by Peter Blaine, Sr., who talked with reservation school teacher Michael S. Adams in 1978 and 1979 about Blaine's long career as a Papago politician. Adams edited tape recordings of those conversations as *Papagos and Politics* (Tucson: The Arizona Historical Society, 1981). When James McCarthy decided to write about his life, he went out and bought a spiral notebook and did it himself. For this work he is unique among all of his kinsmen; James McCarthy's narrative is the first book-length autobiography to be published by a Papago.

A Papago Traveler takes its place, then, among a small but significant group of memoirs and autobiographies which were written by Native Americans. These are a diverse lot. They range from such sophisticated works as Francis LaFlesche's *The Middle Five*

(1900) and N. Scott Momaday's *The Names* (1976) to the sensationalism of the army memoirs of Richard M. Courchene, *Hell, Love and Fun* (1969), and of William Apes' *A Son of the Forest* (1829), a wild, self-published autobiography of a Pequot adventurer who was conscripted into the Army and eventually became a preacher. Taken together, books such as these form a genre which may best be defined by the fact that they force those of us who read about American Indians to question our generalizations about any single image of *the* American Indian in literature.

LARRY EVERS

Going to see the (We-ch) the Kick Ball race

I dont remember how many nights they celebrate them. Grandmother tell me five nights only.

I did not get tired watching them, because I never see Any thing like that before, it was my first time.

I never sleep during the nights. Sun subs. Now up my Grandy brought alone Beans tamales, we eat it for our Breakfast. people had fires all over cooking.

My Great Grand ma', or in papago (Vskob). I stay with her. She is a very old woman. She suppose to look out for me, they say. After they Ceremonies is over we are going home to Get every thing ready to take alone to Iron Stand, and I ask her if its another Dance. She smile and Say no. its going to be a Big Kick Ball race. In papago they Call it (We-ch) the wooden Ball made of Palo Verde tree. and all the people are going over there to see it.

The Ball is little bigger than Base ball. a man can pick it up with his foot or toes while running fast, and kick about 60 ft at the time with his partner, take turns.

Any way we were back home a little field. also other people gone to their home's. Other's going straight to Ironstand they live to far away to go home.

During the day every body getting ready to Leave Iron Stand. fast get Busy Locking every thing up that have Lock's.

Already every body have their things packed, ready for neste day. And see if every things Alright. (Mo-tan) already got the horses near by. and just tie them up for tomorrow.

I was sure Anxious to get going, I never been or seen Iron Stand. mother always told about. And tell us, she live there.

Neste morning every body were up early. it was cold. I was too. I guess every body did not sleep well thinking about the Race. I know I did not sleep awake all night I

They warm up something. But nobody same to be hunger every body think about the race and Anxious as I am to get going. of course I see Boys at home have Kick Ball race's But I never see big man Long distance race with Kick Ball or (We-ch). This old man. Chew-Le-moon. tell me to go to sleep. You will see many people there from many Villages, so you will wide Awake. I just had my eyes close Laying still. I thought the night was the Longest it seames like I was up And went out side, and see Sun light. Others people were getting up.

An unedited page from James McCarthy's handwritten manuscript, begun in the late 1960s.

Introduction

A Papago Traveler is the autobiography of a remarkable person, James McCarthy. In it he tells of his growing up in a Papago home on the fringe of Tucson at the turn of the century, of life in a succession of Indian schools, fighting in World War I, serving a hitch in the Regulars "to see the world," then becoming successively an itinerant laborer, shop worker, mule skinner, farmer, miner, policeman, factory hand, family man, and faith healer.

McCarthy's life was filled with hard labor and the adventures of the real world. He tells of the many people he met in Indian schools, American homes, prisoner-of-war camps, hobo jungles, on a windjammer whose passengers were mostly "junkies," and in factories, fields, and villages. Here are Indians, Mexicans, Anglos, and foreigners. Each he meets on his own level, and he finds good in most of them.

Never once does he tell of discrimination because he's an Indian. Often his race brings him opportunities and friends.

For much of his first fifty-five years, McCarthy lived away from his Papago homeland, but he maintained contacts with friends and his relatives "at home." When he returned to the reservation, he was respected, elected to office, and asked to be a marshal at parades and festivals.

McCarthy writes about the "Big Reservation." This is a large block of some 2,700,000 acres west of Tucson and north of Mexico. James McCarthy was born in 1895 on what became the Big Reservation. Named Macario Antone, he was baptized, he thinks, at the Mission San Xavier. He was soon moved by his parents to the San Xavier area, but, when he was about five, the family built a small hut on the south edge of Tucson. There he lived until age eleven. McCarthy knows little of his parents' background or why, when they owned land and cattle on the reservation, they chose to live in the "white man's country." Wages were poor and the living hard to come by, but the satisfactions must have been greater there.

Though he was surrounded in childhood by "relatives," the traditional Papago system of attributing kinship made it virtually impossible for him to know, or care, which of these were his biological kin. Of his numerous uncles, he can only identify one, José María, as his mother's brother. Figuring importantly in his childhood were Car-me and her husband, Ma-e-tan. He called her "grandmother" in his manuscript but, on questioning, changed this to "aunt," and then to "cousin." In fact, he does not know how to name their relationship in non-Papago terms.

McCarthy seldom speaks of his father. José Antone was an unskilled laborer and was probably away from home much of the time earning the family living. After McCarthy left home for school in 1909, he was never again to see his father, who died in an automobile accident in 1920. José was away working in 1919 when McCarthy returned from World War I. The father did not return to see the son; the son did not seek out the father.

McCarthy's relationship with his mother, however, was closer and more enduring. La-Lee, listed in church records of Mission Station, San Xavier Mission, as Clara, was a domestic worker who had seven children by José. The oldest was José Domingo, born between 1890 and 1892. Macario Antone, later known as James McCarthy, was born in 1895. Other brothers and a sister followed: Nicolás in 1899, then Sarah, Fernando, Grover, and John. Only McCarthy was alive in 1985. José Domingo left home early, but La-Lee tried to keep the rest of her brood close to her while she worked. To Macario, the senior, fell the task of watching the younger ones in the courtyard of his mother's employer. Sometimes he baby-sat at home. About 1917, José Domingo returned to live with his parents and, after the death of her husband, La-Lee lived mostly with Domingo, who remained a bachelor.

La-Lee died of natural causes in 1954. McCarthy

believes that she was 102. If so, she would have been born in 1852, her first son would have been born when she was forty, and she then would have given birth to six more children over the next fifteen years or so. It seems more likely that La-Lee's birth was in the 1870s.

McCarthy's schooling was rather extensive for a Papago in the early part of the century. He had some months at the San Xavier Mission School, part of a year in the Phoenix Indian School, perhaps two years at a school for young Indians in Tucson, six years at the Santa Fe Indian School, another year at the Phoenix Indian School, fifteen months at the Albuquerque Indian School, and then about about half a year once more in Phoenix. He says he reached the eighth grade, but a count of his years in school approaches eleven or twelve. The quality of the instruction was probably not great, and cultural hurdles and frequent moves surely didn't help. His main interests at school were athletics and farm work.

McCarthy entered the National Guard in 1917 after he was rejected by the other services because of size. As an Indian, he was not subject to the draft and his volunteering can best be explained by his love of adventure and thirst for travel. In any case, the discipline and group living of the Indian schools made for few adjustments on entering the service. McCarthy had had the equivalent of basic training in the Phoenix Indian School corps—which was fortunate, because he was immediately sent to Naco, Arizona, for border duty. While still in state service, he participated in the roundup and expulsion of the Wobblies from Bisbee. Shortly thereafter his Guard unit was federalized and moved to California to train for war.

Always eager for adventure, McCarthy volunteered in early 1918 to go overseas as an infantry replacement. He was assigned as a filler in the 28th Infantry Division on July 22, 1918. The 28th had taken heavy casualties a week earlier in the Second Battle of the Marne. Now it was replenishing its ranks and moving forward to help eliminate the German salient on the Ourcq River. McCarthy was at the front for about ten weeks, although part of that time he was in military hospitals as a result of being gassed. Then, while on patrol, he was wounded by a grenade and taken prisoner. The shortness of McCarthy's combat service is not unusual. Most combat soldiers in the 28th Division lasted only hours or days before they were casualties.

From a prisoner-of-war camp in Rastatt, Germany, McCarthy sent one reassuring letter to his mother. It was read to La-Lee by Mrs. Janette Woodruff, a matron with the Indian Service. After the Armistice, McCarthy was returned to the American Army, and a medical report listed his health as good. There were additional months in Europe involved in training and athletics. The men who survived the war had their pictures taken for the Division history. McCarthy's photo shows a serious young soldier who displayed dignity and confidence. The Army eventually sent his division home, but McCarthy did not receive a Purple Heart Medal for his injuries until 1976.

On the day of his discharge, May 8, 1919, McCarthy enlisted for three years in the Regulars. He debated assignment in Panama or the Far East and finally selected the latter. He had a visit in Arizona before starting overseas again. There followed three years of happy, peace-time service in China and the Philippines. One might have expected him to become a career Army man, but thoughts of home and family persuaded him not to re-up. Once back in California, however, he made no effort to visit or contact his family for two years.

Leaving the Army didn't cure McCarthy's curiosity or wanderlust. He moved about in California as a migrant laborer and railroad worker. It wasn't a lack of adjustment that caused his moves; it was the seasonal nature of his employment and his desire to see new places. He was happy almost everywhere.

Eventually, McCarthy returned to Arizona to see his family and, once there, he decided to stay. He helped to harvest a cotton crop, then spent several months visiting the Big Reservation and renewing friendships. For a time he worked in the copper mine at Ajo, but repeated injuries convinced him to return to agricultural work in California. From there he went to Alaska on a windjammer to work in a salmon cannery, and followed this with work among the Yakima Indians in Washington and Oregon.

Out of work in 1929, McCarthy returned to Arizona and soon took a wife. His union with Emilia Castillo was about as coincidental as most events in his life. When he reached his mother's home, Emilia was there. Emilia had been born a Papago in a branch of the tribe left on the Mexican side of the border after the Gadsden Purchase. She had lived for a time in Ajo and was now in central Arizona picking cotton and sharing the family home. As McCarthy and Emilia grew fond of one another, mother and family pushed things along. McCarthy took Emilia on a brief trip to Phoenix in 1929 and, when they returned, his mother and brother had moved out. McCarthy and Emilia simply continued to live together happily for another fifty-five years.

A new phase of life now began. McCarthy became a successful farmer and a settled family man. When irrigation water for his crops was no longer available, he moved his family to Ajo, where he was employed in the mine shops and later as a company policeman. His job was to combat drunkenness among the miners and, while he had considerable success, the job often required him to lock up his friends. The resultant stress made him ill and brought a decision to leave Ajo and take his wife and two sons for another sojourn to California. Before leaving Arizona, he made a stop in Tucson. Emilia wanted their marriage "blessed" and, on June 4, 1944, a ceremony was held at the San José Mission Station, a Tucson branch of the San Xavier Mission. The church records carry a notation of "Convalidatio," that is, the solemnization of an existing union. McCarthy was forty-nine; Emilia's age was given as "about forty-two."

When the McCarthys arrived in California, the defense industries were already going into decline and many factories were closing, even though the war had a year to go. McCarthy worked in several plants, and finally secured a permanent job at the Long Beach naval shipyard until it, too, closed in early 1950. He then returned permanently to Tucson.

While in California, McCarthy suffered from ill health until a neighbor introduced him to faith healing through the publications of William H. Walter, a writer who had once been a Christian Scientist. Faith healing has had an accepted place in Papago culture and McCarthy had no reluctance in trying the Walter Method. Through it, he found recovery for himself and then he was able to help others. Four decades later McCarthy was often seen carrying a much-worn copy of Walter's *The Pastor's Son.*

When he returned to Tucson in 1950, McCarthy erected a small Papago home on the edge of the San Xavier Reservation, close to schools for his sons. Then he took a job at the Geronimo Hotel in Tucson where he was the maintenance man for seven years. His sons, Edward and Joseph, matured and left home to join the services. The house was now too quiet for Emilia, and she welcomed McCarthy's decision in 1957 to retire. Together they built a modest home brick-by-brick, and thereafter they worked their small garden, watched television, tended grandsons, and took trips to revisit many of the places where McCarthy had gone to school and worked.

A nurse came regularly to visit the McCarthy grandsons and soon began to converse with McCarthy about desert foods and his adventures. One day she said, "Why don't you write the story of your life?" McCarthy bought a thick, spiral notebook and each evening wrote several pages of stories he remembered—mostly in chronological order. Once episodes were written he did not change anything. He continued writing for over two years. When his story reached his retirement, he continued on to write a travelog of current family trips and then added several incidents which had not come to mind earlier.

As a military historian, I first met Mr. McCarthy in 1983 after learning of his Army service. His verbal accounts reminded me of my grandfather, who was a great storyteller and a man whom I greatly respected. I recorded and transcribed conversations with McCarthy over a period of five months. He was always pleasant, but reserved; then one day he confided that a decade before he had written "a book" about his life. The narrative which follows is essentially the one which McCarthy wrote in his spiral notebook.

My goal in editing the work has been to employ minimum change to improve the readability of the text and to retain absolutely the integrity of McCarthy's story. A sample page from the original manuscript, in McCarthy's own hand, is illustrated on page xii.

The spellings of proper names often change over the years. The Chinese and Philippine cities are recorded as the author knew them. In addition, in order to retain the flavor of Mr. McCarthy's own words, traditional Papago family names and place names have been transcribed as they were written in the original manuscript. I am indebted to Ofelia Zepeda, of the University of Arizona, for providing here the new orthography for such names:

Traditional Spelling	Modern Spelling
Be-tas-coo-a-wa-tam	Ge Taşcu E-wuadam
Cally	Kali
Car-me	Ka:lme
Chew-Lo-Moon	Celomun
Con-nee-Law	Choni:la
Ha-sa-kit	Hasa:gid
Klamaka	Komelik
La-Lee	Lali
Ma-e-tan	Ma'etan
Mo-M-La-Le	Momlali
Now-a-Chew	Nawaicu
Pan Tak	Ban Dak
Val-Leea	Vali:a
We-ch	We:ch

I experienced some difficulty in trying to locate documentary corroboration of Mr. McCarthy's narrative. School and Army records were scattered throughout record centers in several states, and some had been lost in fires. Fortunately, Mr. McCarthy had kept a number of documents which were useful in pinpointing many dates and places in the narrative. Important confirmation for several incidents can be found in Janette Woodruff's book, *Indian Oasis* (Caldwell, Idaho: Caxton Printers, Ltd., 1939). The most conclusive corroboration for McCarthy's narrative is in the snapshots which he has taken since 1919 and kept in his photo album. They show many of the incidents and places he described in his manuscript and they revealed place names for which I had previously searched in vain.

One of the most intriguing questions raised by McCarthy's manuscript concerns names. Why did Macario Antone take such a variety of names—José Miguel Antonio, Tony Antone, Joe McCarthy, James McCarthy, and others? Part of the answer lies in the different conception that many Indian tribes have traditionally had toward the use of both tribal and baptismal names. In addition, there was the difficulty that many officials had in understanding or pronouncing a non-English name. Mr. McCarthy explained, for example, that his present last name was the result of a recruiting officer's not having heard his baptismal names correctly when he enlisted in 1917: on hearing "Macario," the sergeant wrote it the way he heard it—"McCarthy." Where the "Joe" came from remains unexplained (perhaps from the English version of his father's—or brother's—name, José), but from that time on he was Joe McCarthy to the Army. Sometime after he left the Regulars, he changed his first name to James. So it is that the man baptized Macario Antone became known as James McCarthy.

In the course of editing, some stories were condensed and others expanded. The expansion, which came from conversations with Mr. McCarthy, served to round out incidents and to build the short chapter on the retirement years. The story of acquiring the McCarthy name (in the chapter on the Army years) and the story of his ancestors beckoning to him, McCarthy also told to reporter Dan Tortorell, and versions of these incidents appeared in the *Tucson Citizen* in 1982. Mr. McCarthy was an active participant in preparing the manuscript for publication and carefully read and reviewed the edited version of his story.

In 1985, at almost ninety years of age, Mr. McCarthy was still erect, a handsome man of 5' 6" or 5' 7", who weighed 140 pounds. His weatherbeaten face showed many years of outdoor toil. His mind was keen, he had a dry sense of humor, and he chuckled over a joke. I hope that the reader of McCarthy's story will find in his odyssey an understanding of a quiet, dignified, and thoroughly likable man who traveled to many places and lived successfully in different cultures.

I am grateful to Larry Evers and Bernard L. Fontana, both of the University of Arizona, who have given a number of helpful suggestions and who have encouraged the preparation and publication of this book in numerous ways.

JOHN G. WESTOVER

The Early Years
1895 – 1906

My father was José Antone, my mother, La-Lee. At the time of my birth, they were living in Littlefield Village on the Big (Papago) Reservation. Few families lived in Littlefield in 1895 but there were three nearby villages; the largest was Santa Rosa and the others were Ak Chin and Anegam. Most of these village people were my relatives. My folks were never baptized in a church—somebody gave their names to them as the old people did in the early days.

I was born October 16, 1895. Mother said that occurred after the people came back from worshiping in Magdalena, Sonora. My mother stayed home that time. My parents had lived in other villages—Cally (Circle Going), Pan Tak, and Iron Stand. Our people kept moving around from village to village in those old days.

In my first year, my parents brought me to the San Xavier Reservation, where my grandparents lived on a

1

farm on the edge of the Santa Cruz River just east of the Mission. In the same year they baptized me at the Mission and gave my name as Macario Antone. All Papagos get Spanish names. When I went to school, somebody—my uncle, I think—listed my name as Joe. Then during World War I Mrs. Woodruff, a government matron who was helping my family, wrote to me in France as James, and eventually I took that name. My last name came about because the white people misunderstood "Macario" and changed it to "McCarthy." I've used many names in my lifetime.

I first remember when I was about three years old. I remember that my grandparents grew many things in their fields—like beans, peas, corn, wheat, and canes. The first thing which I learned to like was watermelon and other melons. At that time there was plenty of water to irrigate their plants. They had their own dam on the Santa Cruz River. In those days we had plenty of rain; sometimes it rained for several days. Our people built dirt dams all along the river. One was east of where the interstate highway bridge later crossed the river.

When I was five years old, I used to walk along the river with my older brother and uncle. On each side of the river it was all swamp, and water drained into the river from both sides. The mesquite trees were thick and large. By 1968 we could only see big stumps standing among the new trees. For many years the trees had been chopped down by our people and sold to the people in Tucson. Early every Friday there would be a line of wagons looking like ants going to Tucson. Now I do not think anyone has a wagon and the horses are almost gone.

James McCarthy's homeland in southeastern Arizona, as it was in the early decades of the 1900s, showing the places of his youth on the Big Papago Reservation near Tucson, and the area around Phoenix where he traveled and lived in later years.

In those early days it rained plenty. The flood waters would run over the dams and many fishes would wash out to Tucson. At that time there was water in the stream toward Tucson. I remember when I was a little older that along with the other boys I used to go to the first dam and throw rocks at the fishes. Our folks didn't seem to like the fish—never ate them.

One day my brother asked Mother to show us the four dams along the river. My uncle also went along, and we walked through thick weeds on a little trail toward the first dam. There I saw many fishes, and my uncle and my brother, José, threw rocks at them. We stopped soon and did not go to the other dams. I used to play with other small boys in the river. Sometimes the yellow jackets would come after us when we had no clothes on. If we got stung, then we'd put mud on the sting.

During the rainy season the fields would be flooded and the plants covered with water. The people who lived in the fields would move to high places to the east, where they had other homes. Sometimes the fields would be covered with water for many days. In those years everything looked green. In the spring the wildflowers were everywhere—on the hills and mountains. They were of all kinds, all colors—orange, purple, red, and white. It looked very pretty.

We lived with my grandparents on their farm. Another family also lived with my grandparents. Their name was Mamaka, and they had a house in the field and another on the high place. He was a native of Sonora—a Papago—and they knew many Papagos living on the other side in Mexico. They had two grown sons and a daughter. We were raised with this family. The old family homes at San Xavier are gone now and new families have made their homes around there.

In 1896 my oldest brother, José Domingo, went to school at the Mission where the sisters taught the Indian children. I was a little boy, and he already seemed big to me. I don't know when he left the sisters' school—I was too small to know. I had grown up a bit when a new brother came; he was baptized at the Mission and named Nicolás.

When I was about five years old, my parents had not sent me to school. Then one day the big Papago policeman, Hugh Norris, came and told my folks that I had to go to school. I was scared and didn't want to go, but my parents took me to the Mission School. Inside the one-room school, all eyes turned on me. I saw some of the boys I knew smiling at me, and I felt a little less afraid. It was hard for me to learn. Some of the boys had been there for quite a while and had not learned much. I went there almost a year, and I don't know if I learned anything there at the Mission school.

In 1901, my parents moved to Tucson to look for work, so I had to leave school. My uncle José María took us on his wagon to Tucson. In those days I had never seen a streetcar, train, or automobile. My uncle told me about them so I was anxious to see them.

The town seemed a long way and the wagon was slow going. My father had built a brush house and we moved in. It was in the desert then, no streets; the house was near the place where later 26th Street and 10th Avenue intersected. My other uncle, Benito, was living somewhere around there, but we did not live long in that place. I guess my folks did not like the location.

My father then built another brush house farther east, where 29th Street and 6th Avenue were later. It was a single, rectangular room of about ten by eighteen feet. Everyone lived in that room, sleeping on the floor in the winter and outdoors in the summers, as Papagos had always done. There was a fireplace in one corner for heat, but cooking was done outside. There was no privy—family members just walked out in the wash and did what was necessary.

We lived close to the Nogales Road and we could see the stagecoach, pulled by six horses, passing every day. I guess it was going to Nogales. My brother Nicolás and I used to get up early to see the stage drive by. We would stand behind our brush house, where it was warmer. We would wave our hands to the people and they would wave back.

As I remember, the end of town was on 18th Street, and further south was nothing but bushes. There was a little school on 18th and there was high ground at the end of Meyers Street. Mexican boys had a ball ground on this high ground and we used to go watch them play there every Saturday and Sunday. It was quite a way from our home, but we didn't mind.

About two hundred yards south of the ball ground was an adobe corral where the dog catcher, Cuate, kept dogs, cows, horses, donkeys, and other animals that had been caught running loose in Tucson. I did not know Cuate's real name. One day in 1968, as I was having my hair trimmed at a barber shop, there was an old Mexican man talking about old times in

Tucson when everything was cheap—a haircut was twenty-five cents, bread ten cents a loaf, and so on. The barber asked me if I had been around at that time. I said I remembered a little about old Tucson— how it looked in my young days. I said I remembered the dog catcher and I tried to write his name, but I was not sure it was right. So the barber wrote it on a piece of paper. His real name was Lorenzo McCormick—but everyone called him Cuate. He had a handlebar mustache and a scar on his face.

My uncle Juan, whom the Papagos called Jack Rabbit, worked for Cuate. Cuate carried a pistol and had a rope to catch dogs. Juan, or Jack Rabbit, drove the old cage wagon to throw the dogs inside. Sometimes my uncle asked me to help them drive the wagon, which was pulled by two donkeys and went very slowly. Many times dog owners would get mad at Cuate when he told them they had to bail out their animals. Cuate was very good to us. He gave me a little burro and a dog which nobody claimed. Boys would come and ride the little donkey every evening when we got home from town.

My folks worked every day. I had to go with them to look after my little brothers and (later) sister. My mother and father both worked for a lady called Mrs. Fia, who had a big house. I think Mrs. Fia had a store in town selling women's hats and other things. Her home was just across from the St. Augustine Church, and in 1968 there was just a part of that home still standing.

We had a long walk from our home to town. There were no streets where we lived in 1901. Many of our people lived around there. One village was near the old Southern Pacific roundhouse—later 17th Street and 18th Avenue. Those Papagos mostly came from Comobabi Village on the Big Reservation. Another group was located where 27th Street and 10th Avenue were later.

Most of the Papago women worked for Mexican people, and they understood the language; my mother and father spoke good Spanish. Most Indian parents had to leave their children all day, and they told their children stories about the bad things which would happen to them if they went far away. The parents were afraid for their children. The children listened and would always look out if somebody was coming their way. They would run and hide in arroyos or bushes.

At that time there were not many schools for Papagos, so few children went to school. None of their parents had gone to school and they didn't know the white man's ways and didn't understand their talk. Most Indian boys and girls just ran around and played all day. All boys and girls liked to run foot races and play kickball. The girls played *toka*, a kind of hockey with sticks. They played hard and were often hurt.

At night, the kids would meet somewhere in the arroyo and talk things over—what they were going to do tomorrow. The oldest boy was always the leader, or chief. Everybody loved to go to the mountains and hunt little game with bow and arrows. Every boy had a bow and also a sling shot. I didn't often get to go with them because I had to look after my baby brothers and sister—today they call it babysitting.

The boys sometimes had a kickball race using a wooden ball which was as big as a baseball and made of palo verde wood. The boys were good runners in the old days, long distance runners. Nowadays they are too lazy to run. In the early times the older people taught the kids to get up early and run before they ate. They said if the Apache, our enemy, should come after you, you could outrun them. That was how folks trained their kids in the old days. They told them the story about an Apache raid on Iron Stand that happened while most adults were working in Mexico. The Apache killed the very young and the old, burned the village, stole the horses, and carried off the young girls to the San Carlos Apache homeland.

My mother told me the Iron Stand massacre story frequently, for it was in her village where it occurred. She often told of María, a young Papago girl, who was taken to an Apache village, but she escaped. After many adventures and hardships she made her way back home. When I was young I met María, who was then an old woman.

In 1902 I made a trip into what later became the Big Reservation. One day Mother told me that a cousin, Car-me, had asked to take me with her to Cababi Village. At first Mother did not want me to go; however, I liked my cousin very much and I wanted to see the country, especially my birthplace and how it looked.

Mother cleaned me up to get ready, and my cousin told me when we would leave. When the day came, mother took me to Car-me's home somewhere near 27th Street and 10th Avenue. Car-me's husband, Ma-e-tan, had already brought six horses from the Big Reservation because they could not keep the horses around their home. There were no saddles, but each horse had a home-made carrying frame. Sacks were loaded on so that a person could ride. Some of my girl cousins also went on the trip. I rode with Ma-e-tan.

I do not know what month it was, but it was getting cooler each night. I asked Car-me later, and she said the old people called it Yellow Month. I still did not know what she meant. Anyway, we left Tucson and followed the little trail that we kids used to walk to the mountains and which years later became 29th Street. Many times we walked that trail to the mountains where we would hunt, or pick cactus fruit and prickly pears, or gather flowers to sell to the Mexican people. Where our horses walked later there was a colored people's settlement—our people called it Little Africa. In those days there was a dam just north of where 29th Street was later; there was little water in the Santa Cruz and no bridge.

We crossed the little river near where the freeway came later. Mesquite trees were thick as far as Mission Road. It was all green. Ma-e-tan knew the trail over the hills and the large mountain which our people called Cloth Laying Mountain. We passed over the mountain and down to where later there was Ajo Road. It was empty land but later there were homes built all over the desert.

Our horses were going very slow for they had heavy loads. When the sun was almost down, we came near a ranch that the Papagos called Clear Desert Ranch. It had an old, broken-down windmill with mesquite trees all around. We stopped there for the night as all our people did when going and coming to Tucson.

That night was windy and cold. Every girl helped cook the meal. I could not sleep for thinking about the places where I was going and imagining how they would look.

Next morning Car-me got up early to build a fire to warm up something. I don't remember what we ate, but it wasn't ham and eggs! We could see things a long way—just grass, tall and plenty. When the wind blew, the tall grass waved back and forth like wheat at home at the Mission. Our people used to cut the grass, make bundles, and bring it to Tucson to sell. People used to feed it to horses.

They loaded the packs on the horses and we left. We travelled until sundown as far as Pan Tak. I did not know Pan Tak Mountains or the village. I did not know how far we had travelled that day—I guess not very far with the heavy loads. We had stopped often to rest the horses. Again, it was getting cold at night.

The trip seemed awfully long; it was slow going on those horses. I wanted to ask Car-me how long before we would reach the village. I finally asked her, "How far is Cababi?" She said, "One day. Tomorrow night we reach home," and she pointed toward the mountains due west.

It was rough going over hilly trails the next day. We passed a village called Crow Hang and kept on toward a big mountain. We went on the north side of the mountain and passed another village high on its side—called Comobabi. From there it was not so far, but the trail was rough, going up and down over hills, arroyos, and rocks to Cababi. The sun was down and the horses moving slow. We finally reached the village as it was getting dark. I was glad we had finally reached Car-me's village and glad to get down. It was a tiresome ride on horses because I had never ridden a long distance on a horse before.

It was my first time in Cababi Village. Next morning I was up early to see how many houses were around here. The village ground was not level and I saw many adobe houses scattered nearby. Car-me's house was near a hill. The village well was at the bottom of a hill in a wash. I saw a cowboy at the well. He drew out water using a big canvas bucket pulled up by a horse. He didn't get off, but another man stood by to empty the water into the trough. That well was still good in 1969. They had installed a windmill, and later they bought a little electric pump.

Car-me's mother, named Vekol, lived in Cababi Village. She was old, but she had never been sick and she got around like a young woman. She worked all the time making baskets, straw mats, pottery, ollas, and other things. She was the oldest village woman. She said one day that all the women her age were gone: "I am the only one left." She told me that when my mother was just a little girl she was already an old woman. Vekol passed away many years later, but her great, great, great grandchildren were living on the reservation in the mid-1980s.

I learned to know the kids in Cababi Village and to play with them. We climbed the mountains as all boys did. From that visit I was able to remember how the village looked. At that time they couldn't drive to grocery stores like nowadays. We did not have coffee to drink. We ate chollas and roasted wheat flour, beans, cactus syrup, dry prickly pears, Indian bananas, and many other things which grew on the mountains. I was never hungry.

Car-me had two homes on the reservation. Cababi was her ranch home, where she owned many cattle. The other was in Littlefield, a flat farm area where her people went during the planting and harvesting season. The horses rested while we were in Cababi, but Car-me was getting things together. "Soon we will leave for Littlefield," she said.

Car-me never told me about the big dance they were going to have near Santa Rosa Village — about two miles from Littlefield. It was the village boys who told me about it. Maybe she did not want me to go crazy with anticipation. I found that the kids were anxious to leave and see the big dance. I saw that the other families were getting their horses ready to leave. Car-me was the boss — she told everybody we would leave the next day. That night I could not sleep for thinking about the big dance.

Next morning everybody was up early. Most everything had already been packed the night before. Ma-e-tan brought the horses and started to load. The girls got on horses and I rode with my uncle. The trail to Santa Rosa Village was rough, but it was the shortest way, and everyone travelled it. There is a village called Circle Walk between Cababi and Santa Rosa, and farther west is Covered Wells, near the mountains.

My mother, La-Lee, used to live in Circle Walk and Iron Stand. She told me that a long time ago our people used to look for gold in the sand in a wash near the Big Mountain west of Covered Wells. When they found little gold nuggets, they would take them to Tucson to trade. The people did not know how much the nuggets weighed or were worth—and maybe they were cheated.

Anyway, the horses walked half the distance, and then we rested them. I think it was about noon, because that sun was hot. Each of us got off. When the sun had gone down some, everybody got on again and we started off. The horses walked very slow. It was dark when we arrived at Littlefield Village, but the horses knew their way home in the dark. I guess everybody was glad to get off the horses because it was tiresome to ride on packs.

People came out to see us, and Car-me introduced me to some old people: "This is La-Lee's son." I did not know them but I learned that this couple were Mother's relatives. They took me into a round, grass hut. The door was low, about three feet high, and they had to crawl in on their knees. I was small, but I had to bend down to go through the cloth door. It was very warm inside.

Next morning the women were up early to cook something or unpack the bags. I had nothing to unpack. Car-me had four daughters, no son; later she had a boy named Fernando. I was also up early and started to inspect the village. I could see that not very many families lived there. I was a stranger to all these people, but I found that they remembered my mother. I soon learned to know them and I played with the boys.

My relatives started their harvest of wheat, corn, pumpkins, beans, and watermelons. Every day I ate melons. I liked that. Car-me introduced me to a big man—his name in Papago was Chew-Lo-Moon, or something like that. He acted as a clown in the harvest dance which was performed every five or ten years. He got out his clown, or Now-a-Chew clothes to clean them and he showed them to me. He had a feather hat, tomahawk, and bow and arrows, all in a coyote-skin bag. He said, "When you grow up, you might wear these. I'm getting old. I'll have to have somebody take my place. Maybe I'll turn it over to you." He laughed.

Later a man came to the village. I knew him because he was married to one of the daughters of my cousin. People nicknamed him Sharp Money; in Papago his name was Mo-M-La-Le. Everyone on the reservation knew Sharp Money because he was a very good dancer. The Yaqui called this dance the *pascola*. One evening, Chew-Lo-Moon asked me to call Sharp Money to his hut. When Sharp Money came, Chew-Lo-Moon asked him to take over as Now-a-Chew, or clown. He told Sharp Money, "I am getting too old to play clown." I think he was about fifty years old. At first Sharp Money did not want the part. Later he changed his mind and next day he came over to try on the clothes. Old Chew-Lo-Moon explained to him how to act. "Do not talk in your mask. Use sign language (hand motions) to people."

When the day of the harvest dance arrived, people came from everywhere—on horseback and in wagons loaded with families. I did not know the villages they came from. We went later than some, as Car-me wanted to stay near our home because there were so many strangers around. That evening we walked about two miles to the dance place. Some people rode horses, but we did not mind; our people were used to walking.

At the dance place, families were camping and cooking. There were fires everywhere. I saw hundreds of people, some sitting, others standing around in circles. We sat close to the marker line with Vekol, who was to look after me. The people were anxious for the show to start.

In the middle of the area was a big, square cornstalk fence about six or seven feet high. Inside, the people who would take part in the ceremonies were getting ready to come out. Everybody was painted and dressed up. Outside were three pretty girls, sort of beauty queens, who stood up all through the festival. One of my cousin's daughters was among them.

The first bunch which came out were about forty young boys, ages from ten to thirteen. All had painted bodies and were swinging something which made it sound like a singing windstorm. They were followed by big men who looked like soldiers in two lines, with their bodies painted in different colors. Each wore a *kora* mask that looked like a strainer—it had little holes all over. They sang and danced. They held an ear of corn in each hand and they rubbed the ears together. I had never seen anything like that before, and I sure liked to watch them. More groups came out after these men. They dressed differently and were without masks. They lined up like dancing girls, had on white men's shoes, painted their bodies, danced and sang, and carried *kora* rattles for keeping time. It was beautiful singing.

As we were sitting on the sideline with Car-me and other people, a Now-a-Chew clown came to where we sat. I was scared because he looked dangerous. He wore a mask, had a painted body, and pointed a tomahawk at me. There were other clowns walking among the kids, scaring them. We could not tell which one was Sharp Money. Some clowns had long spears. They made a motion to people with their hands as they went among the crowd just to make them laugh.

Another group was all women. They were all dressed in different colors, and their faces were painted. Thirty of them lined up in single file, each carrying on the top of her head a basket filled with different desert foods, liked dried cactus fruit and prickly pears. These women sang and danced all around.

The show went on all night. Very late, a man came out carrying a big ball, like the globe, with a little bird perched on top. I learned that the bird was on the North Pole. This man made the world himself. His body was inside it and he was singing. I asked Car-me what the song was. She said, "A Papago legend about a flooded world. Everything was washed away. Only the bird was saved." I guess the white men call the bird a swallow—the man was singing a swallow song. This man had no education in English; he only knew Papago. Our people called him Ha-sa-kit, which means In Middle.

It was a cool morning. Near sunrise I saw the sky-line getting red in the east. One more man came out at the same time as the real sun was peeping out. As the man-sun turned the corner of the fort-like corn-stalk fence, Car-me said to me that the "sun" came around. It was a round ball, red, and about seven feet high. His body was inside and he walked very slowly all around. The "sun-man" our people named Be-tas-coo-a-wa-tam, meaning Acting Like Sun. This man also lived in Littlefield, but I did not know that that was him. As he walked, the real sun came up over the mountains. That was the last of the show.

The sun was now up, and people had fires all over for cooking. Car-me had brought along bean tamales, which we ate for breakfast. Car-me told me they would celebrate five nights only. I did not get tired watching the dancers because I had never seen anything like that before. I never slept during those nights.

Car-me's mother, Vekol, looked after me. She said, "After these ceremonies are over, we are going home to get everything ready to take along to Iron Stand." I asked her if there would be another dance. She smiled and said, "No, it's going to be a big kickball race."

After the dances we returned to Littlefield. Some people left for their homes; others went straight to Iron Stand because they lived too far away. But all of the people were going to see the race.

During the day everyone got ready: things were packed and Ma-e-tan brought the horses nearby. I was sure anxious to get going, and the last night I guess nobody slept well for thinking about the race. Chew-Lo-Moon told me to go to sleep, but I just kept my eyes closed and lay still. I thought that night was the longest ever.

When it began to get light, I was up and went outside. Everyone slept outside on the ground, as they always did, for our people did not use spring beds. People were picking up their bedding, and the women

were building fires to cook something. When breakfast was ready, the family sat down in a circle with
the food in the middle. Each person had a home-
made bowl, but no fork or spoon. We used hands and
fingers. That morning nobody seemed to be hungry
because we were thinking about the race and anxious
to get going.

Our party included three families. The big man,
Chew-Lo-Moon, had a burro, and all the ladies had
horses; everybody rode. We started off in single file.
Iron Stand was about twenty-five miles away, but the
country was rough and the going slow. We travelled
half the way and rested the horses. The sun was hot,
but the Papagos are used to heat and did not mind it.
We arrived when the sun was on one side. I was anxious to see Iron Stand because my mother used to live
there and often talked about it. I saw that there were
already many people everywhere around. At night the
campfires were all over and smoked as people cooked.

I saw many horses and cattle inside the fence; there
were many wagons and much grass. In a hut were
stored the things people were going to bet on the
race — saddles, harness, guns, clothes, money, and
many other things. A man guarded the place, standing beside the door because there were many valuable
things inside. There was not enough room for all the
stakes, so they piled them outside on the ground and
covered them with blankets.

The race was next day. Of course, I had seen boys at
home play kickball racing, or We-ch, but never grown
men. The ball was made of palo verde wood, a little
bigger than a baseball. A man could pick it up with
his foot or toes while running fast and kick the ball

about sixty feet at a time. He and his partner took turns. With men, the race was ten miles or more.

After we arrived, Sharp Money wanted to see the track clearing where the race would begin. Some people did not sleep that night, just sat around the fire talking about the race. I guess that I went to sleep because toward morning they woke me up to eat. Everyone ate a little. People were standing around and men were already saddling their horses. Sharp Money asked me to ride with him to follow the runners. When they started the sun was high—maybe it was 9:30 or 10:00 A.M.

At the starting point, I saw four men with painted bodies—two men on each side. Two balls were put on the line. Two men stood about ten feet from the ball, the other men about thirty or forty feet away—ready to take their turn. A man with a white flag started the race.

There were hundreds of people on foot watching. Many men rode on horses on each side of the course to follow the runners. We did, too. Later I learned that there were many medicine men on each side to watch the runners because the excited spectators might harm the other side's runners. We followed the runners a long distance until our horse gave out. We stopped to rest awhile before we went back. Many horsemen were now returning to the starting point.

People were standing around waiting for the runners to show up. The sun was down on the other side—maybe it was 2 or 3 P.M.—when suddenly we saw horses in the distance. It was so dusty that we couldn't see the runners at that distance. Soon we saw one man kicking a ball, and the people from

Ventana began to cheer and holler and wave their handkerchiefs. "That's our man! That's our man!" they shouted. On our side, everybody was quiet. The runner was getting closer. Soon people recognized him—he was from Comobabi Village, and our side cheered for joy! He was the only one running: the other three men had become sick and had been placed on horses.

The losers were now crying, especially the women. They had lost everything—even the horses and wagons needed to take them home. The winners were good enough to lend them their horses and wagons, but they were brought back to them later. Car-me and Ma-e-tan had won horses, cattle, money, and other things. Everyone was sorry for the losers. That was my last, big kickball race. I've not seen another like it in over three-quarters of a century.

The people began to disappear to their homes, and we returned to Littlefield. It seemed like we went faster; we got home by sundown. It was cool. We did not stay long, for in a few days we left for the mountain village of Cababi. We stopped there for four or five days while the horses rested and everything was put in good order.

Now, for the first time, I was getting homesick thinking about my family back in Tucson. Car-me did not have a boy at that time and I could not play with her four girls. I guess Car-me knew that I felt lonely, so she said, "In a few days we are going to take you back to your mother." I was very happy to hear it.

All that time they were getting things in order and packing. The last night I didn't sleep; I just lay there awake thinking about everything at home, my little brother, and the friends I played with. In the morning, I shook hands with the people in whose hut I had slept. I never saw them again for they died while I was far away.

Car-me lived in Tucson and worked for a Mexican family, so she was anxious to get back. We left early and got back in the night of the second day. My mother was happy for me to return because I always looked after my two little brothers and my sister while Mother worked. My father had taken care of them while I was away.

Sometimes when Mother was home, she would let me go with the boys to visit Cabrillo Park. We did not pay to get in; we crawled under a wooden fence. Once inside, we put something in the hole we had made so it would not show. The Mexicans played music in the park every Saturday and Sunday, and some people danced.

There were animals in the cages and they had a baby bear tied up in the open. We always liked to see him. Many people came to look at him besides the Papago kids. After many months, the bear grew up. He was put in a big cage with bars about eight or nine feet high. Now he was mean. One Sunday I saw a man walking too close to the cage. The bear stuck out his paw, caught the man's pocket, and ripped it off. The man just slipped his coat off and let him have it. The bear ripped it to pieces. One Sunday the bear climbed up the iron bars and chased after people. The keeper went after the bear with a shotgun and shot him dead.

In 1950 when I came back to San Xavier Reservation to live, I found things had changed everywhere. There was no more Cabrillo Park; instead, I saw a school where there used to be the gate to the park. Many homes were built in the park area; the town had grown.

One time, in 1902, when the cactus fruits were ripe, my family went to gather them near the Rincon Mountains. Another family camped with us. I don't remember how many were in that family, but there were several sons, big and small. I played with two boys about my age. There was a little stream of water where we played; I never knew the name of that stream, but now I think that it might have been Pantano Wash. My father had made me a pair of cowhide slippers. All our people wore this kind. I wore them while playing in the water, and in the morning Father found them all curled up like tacos. He showed them to Mother and they laughed. Then he put them in the water to straighten them out and told me not to wear them in the water again.

One day after all our parents had been out gathering cactus fruits, they came back to the camp in the evening to find that one of the boys from the other family was missing. I think he was about eight years old. His father looked for him everywhere but could not find him. Next day he looked again and Father helped him. No trace was found, but later they found a horse's hoof tracks some distance away. They believed that somebody had picked the boy up and carried him away. His family felt very bad.

My folks returned home. I don't know if the other family ever went back there again, but my folks did not want to go there after what had happened. Our people knew that bandits lived in a mountain cave somewhere in the Rincon Mountains. We heard long afterward—but I don't know if it's true—that somebody saw an Indian man with the cowboy bandits. Perhaps it was our friend.

While I was back home, Mother wanted me to take some cactus syrup to her Mexican godmother, who lived across the railroad tracks somewhere near where the Tucson High School stadium was later built. There were a few Mexican houses around there, and sometimes she sent me over there to give them something. That day the lady told me to tell Mother to go visit their family's ranch east of town near the Rincon Mountains. Father borrowed a wagon from my uncle at San Xavier. We left Tucson and travelled all day to arrive at their ranch, which was above the Pantano Wash.

The ranch house was big, and inside were many guns on the walls. They had a colored woman cook and I saw many cowboys. Next morning I went to the river and played in the water; there were plants along the stream, and many cows, so the people had plenty of milk and cheese. Both my mother and father spoke good Spanish and I knew some. Our Mexican friends were very good people, but I don't remember the man's name. We stayed a few days and left for home. I remember the man gave Father some dried meat, cheese, and a sack of something. I asked Father what was in the sack. He said, "Tobacco. Don't steal it." He knew that little boys smoked when away from home.

After a few days, my father went to the godparent's home on the other side of town. Their father and mother stayed on the ranch. That day the godparents got word that bandits had robbed the ranch. They demanded the key to the strongbox trunk and the old rancher refused. They hanged him until his wife gave them the keys. The colored cook cut him down, and he was almost dead. This happened only a few days after we left their ranch.

Indian School Days

1906 – 1917

I was eleven years old in 1906. I had not been to school since I left the San Xavier Mission School in 1901. One day I stayed home with baby Fernando, Nick, and sister Sarah while Ma and Dad went to work. Usually I went with Ma, but this time I didn't. That day the big Papago policeman, Hugh Norris, came to our house and asked when our folks would come back home. "When they come home, tell them you are going to school in Phoenix with other boys and girls." I was scared. I did not want to go away.

I told my little brothers and my sister that we would go to Mama and tell her the news about me going to school somewhere. We walked on a little trail to town, where mother worked. I carried baby Fernando; Nick and Sarah walked. It took us quite a while to get there. Ma asked why we came, and I did not want to tell her, but Nick went ahead first and told her. He said that a big, fat policeman came to

26

our house. She asked, "Why?" "He is going to take Macario to school. Mr. Norris will come again soon to talk to you." I said that he told me that I was going to the Phoenix school. I did not know where Phoenix was or how far away. I had never been anywhere far, except for my trip to the Big Reservation. Mother was very sorry. She did not want me to go away, but she could do nothing about it.

Policeman Norris came again to talk to my parents. He was big—I guess he weighed about 350 pounds and was over six feet tall—but he had a little voice for a big man. My folks knew him well because his family lived near the San Xavier Mission. My father told me what Mr. Norris said—I was to be ready to leave in two days.

The children who were going to Phoenix were to travel on the tops of freight cars. Their families could go along if they wished. My mother did not want to go on a freight car, so only my father went with me. When the day came, the family cleaned me up. I did not have nice clothes and, like most Indian boys, I had no shoes. My parents were very poor; they didn't make much money. My father worked for $1.50 a day. Although many things in the stores were cheap, they could not afford luxuries.

When the day came, we all went to town. It was quite a distance to the Southern Pacific Railroad depot from our place. There was a street car pulled by two mules which went as far as 18th Street, but we did not ride, for my father said that we could walk faster than the car. When we arrived at the depot, I was surprised to see so many people. Whole families were going. Then a man told all of the men, women, and children to climb up on top of the boxcars. Father and I followed them. It was my first time on a freight car, but I was not afraid when I saw so many people.

I remember that we traveled all day and into the night. That night I never slept because of the noise and motion of the train. I was afraid that I might fall off. I do not remember what time we arrived in Phoenix, but it was still dark. Early in the morning we were still sitting on the boxcars until someone told us to get down. I was glad to get off.

The school had sent an Indian man, a Papago, for us and the people followed him. There were two flat haywagons waiting, and everybody climbed on. I believe that the school was about five or six miles from the depot, for it took a long time. We arrived before noon and they checked us students in at the office. I don't remember what name my father gave them for me. After that they clipped our hair off. We were ashamed, for we had never had our hair clipped off like that before. Then we went for a shower. They gave us new clothes—blue denim shirts and Levi's pants, and the first pair of shoes some of us had ever had. Before supper time the new boys and girls were lined up like soldiers. It wasn't so bad for the girls because they hadn't had their hair cut. For the boys, all those bald heads on line were a sight. A band played, the flag came down from the tall pole, and we were marched off to eat.

The mess hall was a big room. Boys sat on one side, girls on the other. A man rang the bell, and all of the new boys and girls were still standing after the others sat down. All eyes were on us. The disciplinarian found places for us to sit, but all of us boys with the bald heads were too ashamed to eat. Once we got a little used to the school, we began to feel more at ease. I could not read or write and I knew very little of the white man's language. The school taught reading, writing, arithmetic, and music. They had vocational training, but I didn't learn much.

We had two rifle companies and our commander was Major Grestead of the 1st Arizona Infantry. We had a very nice band with about twenty buglers and drummers. On Sundays we wore special blue uniforms for our parade and inspection. Many white people would come to watch.

The Pima boys were mean to the Papagos. They used to kick us under the table and take our hats away from us and never give them back. The Pima boys called us Desert People. We did not like to be called that — we got mad at them. We thought it was a bad name they called us. After we learned and understood, then we didn't mind it anymore. Later the Papagos changed their tribal name to Tohono O'Odham, or Desert People. As for the Pimas, at home we always called them the River People.

School was tough for us. None of us could speak English, and the boys did not try to learn the white man's talk — instead, they always talked in their own languages outside of the classroom. Every evening after dinner, the new boys would meet somewhere to talk about the happenings of the day. The older boys took charge. Some of the boys complained that they did not like the ways here at school. Some of the boys were homesick; they wanted to go home, but they did not know how far away home was or how to get there.

Some boys of other tribes ran away to their homes.

They were caught, brought back to school, and put in the school jail. The boys were laid on an empty barrel and whipped with a long leather strap. After that they had to work hard on a long tunnel under the mess hall. Sometimes they were put on a ball and chain. The school's rules were strict, and punishment was hard.

After listening to the boys talk, I wanted to go home. About a year after coming to Phoenix, five of us decided to run away. Our leader was Patriso Francisco, my good friend. He was older than the rest of us and he had been in school longer. He was sixteen, I was twelve, one boy was thirteen, and two were ten. One day we met off the school grounds and talked about going home. Pat told us the plan—that we were going to leave after dinner. He said, "At dinner, each of you put some meat and bread in your pockets or inside your shirt." That afternoon the five of us walked away and headed in the direction of Tempe. It was brush country and we walked along the canal. We were afraid somebody might see us and report us.

When we reached a little store, the two younger boys were tired and wanted to turn back. Patriso tried to talk them into going on. He said that when they got back the school officials would know that they had tried to run away. He told them, "They will whip you and put you in jail," but still they wanted to go back. He said, "All right, you can go," and they returned. The three of us left again.

There were few homes along the route we took. It must have been about 6 P.M. when we reached Tempe. We stayed away from the road and went

through the brush—nobody lived along there in 1907.
When we got to the Salt River, it was about two feet
deep. We tried to drink the water but it was too salty.
We went under a bridge and waded through the water
to cool off. By the time we rested on the other side,
the sun was down. We were wondering where we
would eat and sleep that night.

This was our first time to be on our own. We were
hungry and we had no money. We walked along some
railroad tracks outside Tempe until we saw a little
house in a thicket. We were afraid to ask for something to eat for fear they might call the school. Pat
finally decided to take a chance. He told us what to
say if we were asked questions. When we knocked on
the door, a mean-looking man with a long beard
came out.

The man asked Pat where we came from. Pat lied
and said, "Our parents work over there," and he
pointed toward Tempe. He said we lived in the Gila
River Pima Reservation and that we were going home.
I don't know if the man believed him, but he invited
us into the house and asked if we were hungry. Pat
said, "Yes." The man had lots of eggs and he cooked
plenty of them for all of us. After eating, we felt
better. While we ate, he played an old phonograph
which had a big horn on top.

After we finished eating supper, he told us that he
wanted us to feed the chickens after breakfast. He had
many chickens. We sat down to listen to the music he
played. Later, he gave us some blankets and we slept
on the floor. He was kind, but we were afraid that he
might call the school to find out if we were runaway
boys. I think that people got paid for reporting

runaways. So we decided to sneak away in the morning after feeding the chickens while the old man was not looking. We got up early and fed the chickens before the man was up. Then we ran out through the mesquite brush and kept going. We felt sorry to leave the man that way but, at the same time, we were afraid.

We walked on the railroad tracks all morning. At noon we came to where some poor people lived on the other side of the Gila River. Pat said that they were Pimas. We walked to a grass hut and, when an old lady came out, Pat asked for something to eat. She had nothing except thick, Indian, flat bread, made from stone-ground wheat, and baked in hot ashes. The Papago people baked in the same way.

The old Pima lady asked us where we came from. We did not mind telling her the truth—that we had run away from the Phoenix school. "And where is your home?" "We are heading to Tucson where we live with our parents." She said that she was very sorry for us. "It's a long way to Tucson." She wanted us to stay for awhile and rest, but we wanted to keep going. She told us to follow the railroad tracks to a place called Maricopa where there was water. We thanked her for the bread, said goodbye, and then started walking through the desert.

I don't know how long we walked. I remember we were thirsty and the sun was still high. We were used to heat, however, so it didn't bother us much. The sun was on one side when we reached Maricopa, where we found a water tank and a few old, frame houses. We drank water that was dripping from the tank and felt good. We left before anybody saw us — we were always afraid of the white man.

A little farther we lay under a railroad bridge to rest. Each of us slept for awhile, then woke up. The thirteen-year-old boy wanted to go back to Maricopa for awhile, so he left us, but Pat and I continued walking to Casa Grande. There we found another tank and we drank some water. We walked on aways, then rested under a little bridge. After resting, Pat wanted to go back to Casa Grande. "Maybe catch a train," he said. We had already walked quite a way from Casa Grande and, besides, I was afraid of trains. I told him to go ahead. "I am going on by myself." Pat started back. I also started walking and the distance between us grew. He would stop and look back, and I would do the same. Later I could not see him walking along the tracks.

As I was nearing Red Rock Peak, it was about 4 P.M. — and hot. I was wishing for a watermelon and I watched the sides of the tracks. Where there were green spots, I would go and look. In one place my wish came true, for I found two watermelons growing in a place where there had been some railroad construction. I was glad and happy. Right away I busted one — it was red and sweet. I almost ate it all and I was so full that I could hardly walk, so I sat down for awhile. The sun was almost down and I was thinking about where to sleep. I started walking again — carrying the melon. It was heavy, so I said to myself, "It's too heavy to carry. I might just as well eat some." I did.

It was getting dark as I was passing Red Rock Peak.

Then I saw a fire just across from Picacho Peak, and I made up my mind to go over there. I walked through the brush—it seemed like two miles, but I guess it was less. It was very dark then. When I got close, I saw a man standing by the fire with a rifle in his hand. There was a covered wagon and horses tied up nearby. When the man heard me walking and kicking rocks, it sounded like he loaded his rifle.

As I got closer, he spoke in Mexican—"Who's there?" At that time I understood some Spanish words. I told him that I was a Papago boy, and then he said, "Come." I guess he knew from my voice that I was young. He asked me how old I was. I told him twelve years old. "Where do you come from?" I was afraid to tell him that I had run away from school. Then he asked me if I had parents. I said, "Yes, in Tucson."

By that time, another man appeared. I could see now that this man was blind. He asked me if I was hungry. When I said, "Sí," he gave me a plate of beans and a bun. When I finished eating, they gave me a blanket to sleep on. It was summer and not cold. In the morning, I was up early and ready to leave, but they asked me to eat first. Then they made me some lunch to take along. I thanked them for everything and left for the railroad tracks.

I walked all day, for I was anxious to get home. When I saw Frog Mountain, as the Papagos call Mt. Lemmon, it looked close. I did not rest but walked and walked. It's quite a way from Picacho Peak to Tucson (thirty-five miles). I was happy thinking that Tucson was near. But I walked all day, and, when the sun was going down, I was still walking. Finally I saw some houses in the distance—they were old Mexican homes west of the railroad tracks—then a big oil tank on Main Street. It was getting dark as I passed in front of the Southern Pacific depot and walked toward the old roundhouse. I passed the Papago village on 18th Street—it was dark and the people did not see me. My family lived far south of town. I was finally home.

I was afraid to show up at home for fear of what my folks would think and say to me for running away from school. I knocked at the door. Mother opened it and asked me what I wanted. I said nothing. Then she recognized me and she almost cried. She took me in and fed me. She knew I was hungry—I had not realized how hungry and thirsty I was. Our people can stand heat, thirst, and hunger, and we can travel long distances without water or eats. Even so, it had been a long trip for a boy of twelve (approximately 115 miles). Mother did not ask me many questions. I told her the story, how it happened, and that I had walked home from Phoenix in three and a half days.

Once again I went with mother to her work and stayed there all day watching my little brothers and sister. We came home in the evenings. I was always expecting the police, but several months passed and nobody came. I kept wondering about my friend Pat, whom I had last seen near Casa Grande. Then one day I saw him, and after that I would see him in the distance almost every day. Then he disappeared, and I wondered if he had been picked up.

After many months I felt free and began playing around with the boys again. At times we went to the mountains to pick wild flowers to sell to people in town. Sometimes when mother didn't work, we

35

would go to the moving pictures in town. It cost us ten cents each to go in. At times we used to go to the Court House to pick mulberries around the lawn.

Many Indian boys never went to school—they didn't want to or were afraid. I did not know that there was an Indian day school on what was later 25th Street. Few children attended school there—I think about fifteen or twenty boys and girls. I don't remember who sent me to that little, one-room school but some of my cousins were there. I believe the teacher's name was Phillips or McCormack. We studied all morning and part of the afternoon. I had learned a few things at Phoenix, but very little English. It was not so hard for me, and I could read a little better than the others. We did not go home at noon, for some of the older girls cooked and everybody ate there.

I remember especially that there were two brothers, Thomas and Henry Throssell. I guess that Tom was about ten and Henry about seven. They had a whiteman father and a Papago mother. They lived close to the school. After I left the day school, I did not see Tom and Henry Throssell again until 1952. Tom was then a big man working for the government weighing cattle at the Sells Reservation. Henry was a rancher at the San Miguel Papago Reservation. Both were family men with many kids.

After many years, I saw that the day-school neighborhood had changed. Mesquite trees had been thick all over, and there were no streets around there yet. There was an old slaughterhouse, the Wentz Brothers Packing Company. By 1968 it was gone, but the old frame slaughterhouse was still standing. Some of our people used to go there to get things like intestines, hooves, or heads. Sometimes they gave them away. Nowadays, nothing is free.

My brothers and I used to walk on a little trail to the Santa Cruz River to swim. There was a dam and a small lake. A Mexican was always there and he chased us every time; he even did this to the women when they came to wash clothes. Then my older brother, José Domingo, came back home. He had been away for a long time. He did not stay home much in those days. We told him that a man always chased us when Mother tried to wash clothes. We all went again. The man was lying under a tree, and when he saw us, he got up and came toward us with a stick. José did not move. He spoke in Spanish and told him he'd better not chase us anymore. My brother was bigger than the Mexican, and after that he left us alone.

Later at home, José told the family about an earthquake somewhere in California in 1906. He said it was in a town called San Francisco. We didn't know where San Francisco was, or even California. He said he was working outside of town and he saw many buildings burning. Now he was home and he got a job in Tucson as a pipe fitter.

In 1908, I finished third grade, which was as high as the day school went. Another boy, named Venture, also finished. He was older and taller than the rest of the kids. He had also been to the Phoenix Indian School. My family was now told that I was going to go to school in Santa Fe, New Mexico. I tried to have a good time with the neighbor boys before I left. I thought, "Maybe I'll never see them again."

Policeman Hugh Norris talked to me my folks about my leaving. My little brother Nicolás was listening and he cried after Mr. Norris said that I was going away to school. He wanted to go with me, but he was only nine. Mr. Norris said that he would find out if they would take Nicolás. Soon he came back and told the folks that it was all right for him to go. Nicolás was very happy to go with me and he was not afraid.

I don't know what month they told us to be in Tucson. It was hard for us to know the days, months, and years. Father knew that there was no bus to pick us up, so we walked to the corner of Meyers and Broadway. Here was a two-story hotel and they took Nicolás and me to the second floor. There were spring beds for us to sleep on. I thought that we were the only ones going, but later more boys came upstairs. Everyone had a bed. Brother Nick and I slept close together. That night Nick fell out of the bed and cried. I picked him up. Our people were not used to sleeping in beds, for everyone slept on the ground. That night I heard others fall down on the wooden floor. I could not sleep that night for thinking about where we were going so far away.

Next morning very early, Policeman Norris came and woke us up before the sun was up. There were twenty boys and two girls. None of us had anything to carry—no personal things. Mr. Norris marched us to the Southern Pacific depot where we would get on a train. To where? Nobody knew. Few of the Indian children had been away from home and they were wondering how far we were going. Most were afraid. I was glad to see a cousin, Pablo Romo, who was also going. He was a big boy and he said that he would look out for us.

I do not remember how long the train traveled, or the route. I did not sleep much but I watched out the window. My little brother slept soundly all the way. The train stopped many times; it had been going for a long time when they called for us to get off. We thought that it must be the place we would go to school. Everybody was surprised, for there was nothing to be seen from the station except a few houses. Nobody spoke enough English to ask questions. They told us to sit down inside the station. Everyone was asking each other, "Where is the school?" Nobody knew. Later we saw a train coming from the west. They told us to get ready to get on. There were only two cars behind a small engine. They loaded us on. Later I learned that the little station was called Lamy Junction, New Mexico.

Sometime in the evening, we arrived at Santa Fe. It looked almost like Tucson with its adobe houses. Three men were waiting for us—two Indians and a white man. I was surprised when one talked in our language. He was a Papago, and he told us that there was a flatbed wagon to load on. The school was about five miles south of town, out in the desert. One of the older boys asked the man if there were more of our people in the school. He said, "Many of them—boys and girls." Everyone was happy knowing that there were more Papagos at school. Some were from the Big Reservation, even more from San Xavier.

When we arrived, everybody turned out to look at us. Some of the new boys recognized others from home. I was surprised to see Patriso Francisco, who had run away with me from the Phoenix school in 1907. No wonder that I had not seen him the past year. I thought that maybe he was caught. He said not. He had come to Santa Fe in 1908, the year I was in day school. Pat was older now, almost nineteen, and I was fourteen. Once again we were best friends.

As at Phoenix, they marched us away to the big hall where right away they clipped our hair off. They gave us new denim clothes and sent us to the shower. We were all ashamed of our bald heads. In the mess hall, all eyes turned to the new bunch, and that was hard. Some felt so badly that they wanted to die. Everyone was ashamed to eat there, for people never looked at us like that at home.

We new boys began to feel at home after meeting our own people. Some had been there four years and had one more to go. I was started in third grade and I was promoted every year. Some began in first grade. It was hard for them to learn English, for out of class the boys spoke only Papago.

Unlike Phoenix, the Santa Fe school was not formed like the military. But we had no coach or organized sports. On our own, the boys got together and made a baseball team. Every evening we played ball among ourselves. Each boy had a baseball glove — big, like a basket, but with very little padding. They weren't like today's. The catcher had a chest protector, but I didn't wear it and I was never hurt. One of our boys, José Barber, a Papago, was a good pitcher. There were five other Papagos and Nero Talafa, a Santa Clara Indian; Julian Santha, a Navajo; and one boy who was a Piute. Patriso Francisco was the shortstop and I was the catcher. The boys selected me as their captain.

In 1911, when I was sixteen, we boys talked about trying to get a baseball game with some small school team around Santa Fe. Pat talked pretty good English, so he and I went to see Mr. Girllee, our disciplinarian, to try to get us a game. Mr. Girllee was a Mexican who had a German wife and a daughter. The boys had nicknamed him "Cowskin." He said he'd try to help. Mr. Girllee talked to our superintendent, Mr. Clinton Crandall, and soon we were scheduled to play St. Catherine's Catholic School. We won our first game and the boys were happy. Next we played St. Michael's College in town and beat them. We thought that we had a pretty good team.

All students from fourth grade upward were assigned different trades every month—like carpentry, shoe repair, painting, blacksmithing, and farming. In my second year, I chose working on the farm and I liked that very much. My boss was Mr. Robert Anderson, a newcomer who did not take long to marry one of my teachers.

The farm raised horses, pigs, and cows. I helped to milk the cows and I drank plenty of milk. We raised all kinds of vegetables, and in the fall we buried carrots, turnips, and cabbages. We piled straw and dirt over them to keep them from freezing. The boys would steal them in the winter and eat them raw. On snowy mornings you could see boys' tracks where they had slipped through the barbed-wire fence to dig out the vegetables. They also took corn at the pig pen and would roast the ears in an arroyo. There was an apple orchard, and we picked green apples, packed them in barrels, and locked them in the cellar to eat at Thanksgiving and Christmas. At the Indian schools our food and cooking was "white man's" — potatoes, meat, and vegetables.

Sometimes I drove the school stage and took students and employees to town for shopping. While I was there, I would pick up the school mail. When I took the long coach, I would hitch up four mules. I was also one of twenty boys that the school assigned as firemen. We had a two-wheel cart with hose wrapped around it, and every two weeks the boys would pull it at fire drill. Often we would be in our schoolroom when the fire whistle blew and we would run out to the cart.

All of the school employees knew me and sometimes they would ask me to do something for them in their place. I knew the night watchman very well, and, when he went on vacation, he picked me to do his watch for two weeks. I sometimes worked as fireplace man and would look after all of the fireplaces in the student buildings. When I worked for someone else, I got no pay for it. I just liked to help.

By the spring of 1911, like most of the Indian boys, I had forgotten about my home and family. We didn't talk about them much anymore. I hadn't even seen my brother Nick for some time, as he was in the small boys' building. One day I saw him and was surprised that he had grown and was a big boy. He was on the track team, ran the 100-yard dash, and pole vaulted. At school Nick worked as a shoe repairman.

The winters took time to get used to. We came from Southern Arizona, with its hot climate, and

Santa Fe was cold and had lots of snow. The Papago newcomers had a hard time the first winter but eventually got used to it.

At the end of each school year, Mr. Crandall picked forty or fifty of the older boys to work in the Colorado beet fields. In 1911 I was happy to be asked to go. We made about two dollars each day — a little of it was our summer spending money, but most of it was sent to our school. At school we could go to the office and draw out a bit, but we had no school canteen and could not spend much of it.

We made the trip by train. In Rocky Ford there was a headquarters for Indian workers. The employment agent, Mr. Archky, was a big Seneca Indian who had a white-woman wife. There were other Indian-school boys there from New Mexico, Kansas, Oklahoma, the Dakotas, and elsewhere. Mr. Archky would send the boys out to different places — fifteen or twenty to a camp.

Twenty of us were taken to a camp near a little town called Manzanola. I don't remember how many miles it was from Rocky Ford, but I guess it was not too far away. Our camp was out of town and we had tents to live in. Manzanola was a hot place. Working in the fields we had to crawl on our knees thinning beets with a foot hoe. Most of us had never tried that kind of work before, but everybody stuck to his job, even though it was hard on the back and knees. We worked there about three and a half months and then went back to school at the end of August. During all of that time none of the boys went to town. None of them ever got a letter from home and I don't think any of them wrote a letter.

Our group picked a boy to be our cook. Most of us were small—shorties—and he was one big boy, so we called him "Little Boy." We all thought that he was a good cook. He made good tortillas and he cooked beans nearly every day, but nobody complained. One Sunday, the boys were lying around camp talking about going back to school. There was a little pond near the camp, but no one tried to swim there. One of the older boys knew that the water was very shallow—maybe only a foot deep. This boy asked the cook if he could swim. The cook said, "I am a good swimmer." The older boy said that he wanted to see him swim—if he could. The cook took his clothes off, ran to the pond, and dived in. His head stuck in the mud and the boys had to pull him out. The boy had a stiff neck for days, but still he cooked. Everybody was sorry for him and gave him a hand with washing dishes.

The Indian agent came to our camp every week to see how we were getting along. He told us that we would go back to school at the end of August. Everyone was happy to hear it and could hardly wait for the day to come. The sugar beets had grown big and the nights were getting cool. On the day we left, everybody was happy to go—we felt like we were going to our own home. We travelled I don't know how long before the train reached Lamy Junction. There we got on the little train with two cars and were met in Santa Fe by the flat haywagon.

There was a penitentiary about half a mile from school. Sometimes when the school needed bricks, they would send me with a wagon to get a load. I drove a two-mule team inside the pen. The prisoners would load the bricks for me while the guards watched them carefully.

During those first three years, from 1909 to 1911, I felt at home in Santa Fe school. I did not have home-sick feelings because, I guess, I had my mind on work, play, school study, and everything else. I volunteered to help milk cows. The night watchman would wake us about 4:00 A.M. before anyone else was up. We would take from four to twenty gallons of milk to the kitchen. They had me doing everything around there — stage driver, mail carrier, night watchman, fireman, milker, and captain of the baseball team. I did not mind it.

In 1912, I was seventeen. Kids from all the tribes were like brothers now. Those who came here to school with me in 1909 forgot about their parents at home in Arizona. Our parents were poor and could not send us money. Sometimes I thought about my parents and felt badly. However, during the six years I was at school, I never wrote them a letter and I never got one from them. An uncle came one time to see how we were doing at school. He stayed on and worked as a baker.

Early in 1912 those boys who had worked in Colo-rado began looking toward the end of the school year so they could again work in the beet fields of Colo-rado. It was the only time we could make any money and we were happy to have some which we could spend during the school year. My younger brother Nick wanted to work this year, but he was still too young. Many new boys wanted to go and asked "Mr. Cowskin" to put their names on the list.

It was the last of May when we left. We loaded on

the same haywagon to go to town, and we took the little train to Lamy Junction; another train took us to Rocky Ford. The Papago boys liked to ride the trains. The train stopped in a few towns whose names we did not know. When we reached Rocky Ford, the agent met us and marched us to his headquarters to check our names before he sent us to different farms. This year I was surprised: Mr. Archky picked me to work for a Japanese farmer who lived seven miles south of Rocky Ford. The family consisted of the farmer, his wife, and a fourteen-year-old son.

The whole family came to pick me up at the agency office. They were nice people, good to me. Mostly I cultivated the sugar beets — which I already knew how to do from work on the school farm. The farmer had two big horses which pulled the cultivator. They seemed to like my work. The Japanese boy did not speak much English, but we got along very well. In the evenings he tried to teach me Japanese and I learned a few words. I used to repeat them to his mother and she would laugh. In turn, he asked me words in English. He learned more than I did.

While I worked there, I didn't visit Rocky Ford. The boss said that if I wanted anything, his son would take me to town, but I just stayed around their home. Before the Fourth of July, however, the farmer told me that all of us would go to Rocky Ford to celebrate. The town had a fair called "Watermelon Days." In the park were piled watermelons and cantaloupes — thousands of them, and my boss put me in one of the booths to hand out melons to people. When it was over, what a sight! Thousands of melon rinds lying so close together that people could not walk through them. I have never seen such a mess, and I wish that I had a photograph. My boss said that it happened every year.

I worked for that family until the last of September, while most of the other boys went back to school a month earlier. When the farmer got word from the agent that I was to return, he asked me to come back the following year. The family was sorry to see me go. The whole family took me to town to say goodbye. After four months, and as much as I had been a part of the family, I almost cried.

Some of the boys came to town from a long way away and did not arrive until late, so we stayed in town overnight. Few people had automobiles in those days, and for the first time I saw one on the streets of Rocky Ford. It was a small one that made a lot of noise, and smoke came out behind. Next day, after everyone had arrived, they put us on the train. We stopped at La Junta and Trinidad before reaching Lamy Junction and the train for Santa Fe. When we arrived, some boys were waiting for us with a wagon to take us to school.

We were glad to be home and everyone at school was happy to see us. Many small boys came to see me; the boys liked to carry my baseball mask and catcher's glove when I played ball. Everybody seemed to like me. I had many young friends among all the tribes, but I never had a girl friend. I knew the girls in my class, but my interest was in sports. When I went out with a friend, it was always Patriso.

To my surprise, at the beginning of the school term, my older brother, José Domingo, arrived from Colorado. He had been working in Denver and had decided to go back to school. Long before, he had gone to the San Xavier Mission School and later to the Tucson Presbyterian Indian School. After that he went to an Indian school in Grand Junction, Colorado. I hardly knew my brother, for he was not much at home. Anyway, they signed him up and right away they put him in the powerhouse as a fireman. He had had some experience in that kind of work before. That year, Superintendent Crandall bought an automobile. It looked like a carriage with wooden wheels and hard rubber tires. It ran about ten or fifteen miles an hour, which we thought was very fast. The superintendent had my brother José look after it, clean it, and make it shine all the time.

When we came back from Colorado, we missed some of the older boys. They had been at school five years and now had gone back to their homes. Many were from Pueblo tribes in New Mexico. We missed them. I was back at my Santa Fe home again, and the weather was getting colder. It seemed to me that Santa Fe was winter's coldest place. The school had few organized games to play in the winter, and we just sat around and felt cold. They made us stay inside during the bad days, but there was not much heat in the buildings. Cold as we were, we were more used to it and it wasn't as bad as the first year.

I never went to town for myself but often I drove the mail stage wagon and some passengers who wanted to shop. Most of the time I worked around the stables. I volunteered to help the boys milk cows. Sometimes I would take milk to my brother in the engine room.

The school had no football team, so we played a "pick-up" game among ourselves. Thanksgiving came, and all the school children had a big dinner and entertainment in the school auditorium. At Christmas we got plenty to eat and a little show, but there were no presents.

A teacher I knew at the Phoenix Indian School, Guy Gilmore, came to Santa Fe in 1913. He did not remember me, but I remembered him. He was an Apache and had been mean to the small boys — whipped them all the time. He used to say at the Phoenix school, "You boys eat like a hog." Mr. Gilmore played the cornet and at the Santa Fe school he organized a school band. My little brother, Nick, learned to play the cornet.

In the spring of 1913 we played baseball every evening by ourselves. We reorganized our team and I was captain again. I placed each boy where I thought he would play good: my older brother was at first base. I had to do the coaching, as the school did not have a coach. I told the boys, "I think that we are going to make a good team. We ought to get games with teams from other towns." We saw in the paper that the team at Albuquerque Indian School was beating everybody around the state. We told Mr. Girllee that we wanted to play with the Albuquerque Indian School team. I do not remember how long it was before we heard about the game — it seemed a long time. Mr. Girllee finally broke the news: he said that Superintendent Crandall had got us a game with the champions.

Our school did not have money to send us to Albuquerque by train, but Mr. Crandall's son had an old car, and he said that he would rent another car in town. The school had just made us some blue uniforms, the first that our team had. On the morning of the trip, we loaded into the two old cars and left about 8:00 A.M., wearing our blue uniforms. The old wagon road we followed was very dusty as we drove through the desert, and, when we got to the school that afternoon, we were a mess. Right away they took us to the showers and showed us where to sleep. After a shower, we felt much better. We were tired from that rough ride and we rested because the next day we would play the champions.

We really wanted to beat the Albuquerque Indian School team. Their team had all Navajo boys and they were big. The Santa Fe team was mostly Papago and neither tall nor big. Most of our boys were between 5′4″ and 5′7″. I was only 5′4″. Next morning we ate breakfast with the students. After that they showed us around the school grounds—nice school. We had a good rest before the afternoon game, but everybody was anxious to get started. They hauled us to the town ball park on flat wagons. Our players were in fine shape.

A big crowd was on hand to watch the game between two Indian schools. Our pitcher was José Barber. He was good and struck out many men. We had two more pitchers but did not use them. That afternoon we beat the champions 5 to 0. The boys were so happy. After the game, Mr. Girllee sent a telegram to Superintendent Crandall. In the mess hall, everybody went wild. The following day we played New Mexico University and they beat us 5 to 3. Our pitcher's arm got sore but he still wanted to pitch. Anyway, the important game had been beating the Albuquerque Indian School.

We were in Albuquerque for four days playing baseball and sightseeing. One evening there was a party — a dance in honor of our team. I was not much on parties and I couldn't dance. Even though we beat them, they were very nice to us all the time. After four days, we were ready to leave for home. We said goodbye to all the students. Then Mr. Perce, the Superintendent of the Albuquerque Indian School, shook the hand of each one of us. He asked me and some of the other players to come to his school. Once more we loaded into the old cars and were on the dusty trail. I don't know how many hours we traveled, but everything was fine with the cars and we had no trouble. We arrived at school in the evening. We were the happiest boys.

My final year at school was supposed to be in 1913. My little brother Nick, who came with me, was fourteen, and he returned to Tucson. My folks had some cattle on a ranch on the Big Reservation and he went there to help look after them. Even though we had been there for five years, Mr. Crandall talked to the ball team and asked them all to stay. I was not worried about going home. I was glad to stay another year because I liked playing baseball.

That summer fifty boys were picked to go to Colorado and I was going for the third time. I decided that I did not want to work for the Japanese family but that I would stay with the bunch, so that we ball players could play on Sundays. As usual, Mr. Archky met us, assigned us to camps, and came weekly to check on us. Our Santa Fe players got a game with some little farm-town teams. Later, a white-boys' team in Rocky Ford wanted me to play with them. They put me in as shortstop. At that time, I could play any position except pitcher. A colored-boys' team also hired me to play. I sure had a good time that summer. That year was my best in baseball and I thought the three months went too fast.

I returned to Santa Fe on the last day of August for my sixth and final year. There were many children already at school — some new, some old. Others arrived each day. The new kids, and those who had gone to their homes for the summer, had long hair. They never cut their hair at home. The big boys at school who worked as barbers cut the boys' hair, which piled up like a hay stack. The boys who had gone to Colorado did not have to have their hair clipped — we had had our own barber.

Once again the school year was study, work, and play. Thanksgiving and Christmas were special and many families came to visit their children and bring all kinds of sweet bread to them. That spring we had many baseball games with teams from nearby towns.

The older boys were all looking toward the end of May, for they were anxious to go to Colorado. Many new boys went who had not gone to the beet fields before or worked hard on their knees. Again, I stayed with the bunch.

During all of those four summers in Colorado I never went to town just to visit. On Sundays we usually stayed in camp and rested. One time a camp boss came and told us that we could stop work on the Fourth of July and go see the fireworks in Rocky Ford. He said that lots of things would go on in town that day. However, the boys did not want to go. On that July 4, 1914, there was no work and everyone was happy just to lie under a shade tree.

In the morning I thought of walking around to see things nearby. I guess I walked about a mile and came to some railroad tracks. I walked along the tracks to the west, away from Rocky Ford. I was used to walking and running while training at school. I guess that I did not realize how far I walked that morning. After a while I came to a section house. A man came out and asked me if I wanted to work. I asked him, "What kind of work?" He said, "To check the track joints." He showed me how to tighten the joints if I found a loose one. I said, "Yes," without thinking.

I forgot to ask him how much he would pay me. I just took the job. He gave me a three-wheel track car which had wrenches and red flags on the sides, and he told me how far to go. When I left there, it must have been 10:00 A.M. I started to push and pull, and I guess I went too far. Then I began to think: I had no blankets, no food, no cooking pots. The man had shown me a torn-down house where I could sleep. I guess he thought I was a fool. Anyway, I just kept pumping the car until I saw a town. I didn't know what town it was, but about a mile away I pulled the car from the tracks and walked in.

I was hungry, so I found a little store and bought something to eat. I went outside the town and ate lunch under a tree. I rested and I slept. I guess the section man was wondering what happened to me for not showing up. I was also thinking about why I left the camp and the boys. I knew the boys would be worrying about me, because I had never left camp before. I thought about going back to camp; then I changed my mind and decided to hang around and see this town, which I learned was Pueblo, Colorado. I stayed around about a week trying to decide what to do. I thought I was too long gone to return, but I was sorry that the boys would worry about me.

I had a little money with me, but not much. Since all of the money from work was transferred to the school at the end of the summer, I had not been paid. I don't know what ever happened to that money. I thought of finding a job, and one day I walked to a steel mill. I stood and watched the men work the red-hot iron, and then I returned to the place where I stayed under the trees. I slept there another night, and next morning I made up my mind to go home to Arizona.

A problem was that I didn't know which way to go. I saw a railroad track leading south from town, so I followed it. It looked like it was not much used, but I kept on all morning and afternoon. I never saw a single house along the way and I had nothing to eat. Early next morning, about 3:00 or 4:00 A.M., I came to a town. I saw that its name was Raton. Nobody was around yet—it was too early. So I kept on going, following the tracks through mountains and canyons. That evening I came to another town, Las Vegas, New Mexico.

Outside of town, I saw a fire in the brush. A man was sitting by the fire cooking something. He was an Italian. He asked me if I was going to catch a train. I said, "No, I have just walked in from Pueblo." He was sorry for me having walked so far and he gave me some stew. I was hungry, for I had not eaten for two days. He told me to catch a freight train so that I wouldn't have to walk so far. He caught a train toward Colorado later, and I started walking again. Toward morning I reached Lamy Junction Station, where the branch line train goes to Santa Fe. I thought about going there, but I was afraid to show my face, for I had run away from the work camp. Anyway, I had gone to school for six years and would only be going back to Tucson if I returned there. Still, the school was like home and it was hard to forget.

I started walking again toward Albuquerque and arrived there in the evening. I asked myself if I wanted to go to the Albuquerque Indian School. Superintendent Perce had asked me to come to his school that time after we beat his team in 1913. I knew that one of my friends who played with us that year, Nero Talafa, had gone to that school. Nero was a Santa Clara Indian from not far north of Santa Fe. But he might have gone home for the summer, and my clothes were so dirty that I decided not to go like that.

That night, outside of town, I found a vacant house with a high porch. I slept under the porch. In the morning I looked for a store to buy something. I hung around the town for three days. Early on the fourth day, I left Albuquerque, walking again on the tracks toward the west. I stopped at Isleta Indian Village. I knew many Isleta boys at school and thought maybe they would be there. A woman came out—I guess she thought I looked hungry. She said, "Wait." She got a big loaf of bread and gave it to me.

I don't know how long it took me to get to Gallup, which at that time was just a little town. I never stopped long; I kept moving all the time. I walked night and day—seems I never got tired. Some of those little towns I don't remember, except Holbrook. One morning I got to Flagstaff. I didn't feel hungry, but I thought, "I'll buy something anyway." I went toward a store, for I rarely bought things in restaurants. I guess it was about 8:00 A.M.

I saw a lady coming toward me, and I was surprised when I recognized her. Miss Fiston had been my fourth and fifth grade teacher in Santa Fe. I tried to look to one side, but she knew me and called me by name, "José Miguel Antonio." That was the name I used at Santa Fe. Somebody gave me that name—I think it was my uncle. I stopped, and she asked me what I was doing in Flagstaff. I told her that I was on my way home. I did not tell her that I had run off from work in Colorado and walked all the way here. She told me that she was attending a teacher's summer course at the normal college. We talked a bit, and then she left for school. She was a very good teacher, kind to everybody. I'll never forget her.

I started walking again toward Williams. Sometime later a bunch of coyotes came after me. It was a wooded area and I climbed a pine tree. I was scared. I guess I was up there for more than half an hour when a train came along and scared them away. I stayed up there for some time to make sure that they were not waiting to eat me when I came down. When I finally climbed down, I waited for some time close to the tree. I was still very scared.

Finally I started out again and walked to Williams. It was a very small place, few houses. I looked for a store and bought something to eat. Then I walked on to Ashfork. I didn't go near the Ashfork station but passed a little to one side and lay down under a bush. I went to sleep right away, and when I woke up, it was dark. I walked back toward the station. At the junction the tracks separated, and I figured that those which went south either went to Phoenix or Prescott.

I didn't know it then but I had already walked about eight hundred miles. I began thinking about stealing a ride, although I had never done that before. I waited for a long time. "It must be midnight," I said to myself. Finally a short passenger train came — maybe from Prescott. I waited for some time, and a few people got on. I was hiding in the dark and ready to jump on. The train began to move, so I ran and jumped on behind the engine water tank. There was a little step there, very low. Above it was the platform, and I was afraid that the trainmen would see me and push me off.

One time the conductor opened the car door and looked out while holding a lantern in his hand, but he did not see me. Then a second time he came out and stood directly overhead. I tried to sit still, but I guess I moved my head a little. Right away he held his lantern so that the light fell on my face. He said, "Where are you going?" I said, "Phoenix." "You Indian?" "Yes." I told him that I had walked from Rocky Ford and this was my first time to jump a train. I guess he didn't believe me.

The conductor listened as I told my story; then he told me to stay on. He said, "When the train slows down, jump down about a mile from town." I thanked him for letting me stay on. When the train slowed down, I jumped off. It was getting light. From there I walked to town and I learned that it was Prescott. It was still too early, so I just walked outside of town and rested under a pine tree. When the sun came over the mountains, I walked into town looking for a place to buy something to eat. I found a Mexican place and ordered a plate of beans and some coffee. After that, I felt better.

I went to a small park to rest, but I could not sit long. I felt like moving on. I returned to the railroad tracks and followed them through the mountains. Sometime in the afternoon, I reached a little place called Kirkland. There was a little station and a few houses. I saw a fire in the bushes outside of town: it was a hobo camp. There were two men cooking something. One said, "Hello. Where are you from?" I told him that I came from Colorado, walking all the way. He said, "You walked all the way! You should ride a train." Then he told me there would be a train coming about midnight which would go to Phoenix. They gave me some stew.

I waited that night, and, sure enough, a freight train came and stopped to get water. When the train started, I ran to catch it. The car I caught was loaded with lumber. I climbed on top and lay down; I was soon asleep. How long the train travelled I don't know, for I did not wake up until the train was in Phoenix. The sun was already hot when I awakened. I got up and looked about. The car was almost in front of the depot and in the center of the switching yard. I was surprised and scared because I was afraid of being caught by the cops. I tried to think of how to get down without being seen. I would stick my head out to see if anybody was around. There was. About 3:00 or 4:00 P.M. I was still up there like a scared cat.

I was getting tired and I decided to take a chance. First I looked and saw no one around; then I climbed down as fast as I could and ran toward the bushes. I didn't see anybody after me, but I was still scared. I felt like somebody must have seen me—maybe it's the way an escaped prisoner feels. I had heard about the mean railroad bulls who beat up a hobo if they got a chance, and I was glad to be safe.

I walked to the south side of Phoenix where all the poor, lazy men hung around on Jefferson Street. I stood there to see if I would recognize anybody. There were some Indians but I did not know them. They asked me for a dime; I told them that I also needed money.

I walked to Washington Street and it was my luck to see a friend, Juan María. He had left the Santa Fe Indian School in 1910 and he was now a man. He also saw me and smiled. "Where have you come from?" I told him. He said, "You sure have grown up. The last time I saw you in Santa Fe, you were only a boy." He laughed and added that he was now an old man. I guess he noticed my hungry look, and he said, "Let's go eat something." I pretended not to be hungry. "Come on. After we eat, you can tell me your story when you feel better," and he laughed. I said, "All right, but it's a long story."

After we ate, I asked, "Do you work anyplace?" "Yes, I got a job at the Montezuma Sanitarium. I'll take you there." I did not want to go—his boss might not like it. "My boss, Mrs. White, is a very kind woman. Maybe she'll give you a job — she likes to hire Indians. She used to be a nurse at the Phoenix Indian School, and now she owns this sanitarium." I said, "I'll go."

When we left town, we rode on a street car as far as a place called East Lake Park. From there we walked two more miles. The sanitarium was near the State Hospital. Juan was staying in a little, frame house which was just big enough for one man. Juan told me he worked very hard. "I'm the only worker and I have to do everything around here — wait tables, wash dishes, clean rooms, and yard work. I'm glad you came along."

Next morning Juan told the boss about me. He came back and told me that I would start work after breakfast. She told Juan to see that I got a good breakfast, and good meals every day. Mrs. White was a big woman — six feet tall and she must have weighed 300 pounds. Her husband, who was only about 180 pounds, worked as a baker at the State Hospital. Mrs. White asked me if I knew how to wash dishes. I said, "Not in a big place." She said that she would show me how to wash dishes and after that I would make the beds and clean the twenty-five or thirty little houses for the patients. I had no trouble doing these jobs because I had learned at school. I worked hard, as I always do on any job I have. The pay was small but I did not mind it because Mrs. White was very kind to me, as she was to Juan. I worked at the Sanitarium all summer.

When I first came to Phoenix, I changed my name to Tony Antone. Juan knew that wasn't my real name, but he didn't tell Mrs. White when she asked my name. That fall I enrolled at the Phoenix Indian School. It was my second time at that school; the first was in 1906, but they didn't remember me. My name was different and I had grown up—I was nineteen years old in 1914.

I had learned to play baseball and football at the Santa Fe Indian School even though we didn't have a coach. At Phoenix they had a coach— Mr. Vane. When he found that I could play baseball and football, he quickly put me on the teams. The school had good teams. I especially remember two players, Clarence and Frank Butler. They were brothers—half-Indian, half-colored—and very good athletes.

The school year went quickly and, when summer vacation came, I again worked for Mrs. White. During that summer I began to think about the Albuquerque Indian School where we had played the champions. I thought that I would like to go to that school because it was different from the Santa Fe and Phoenix schools. To go to Albuquerque I would have to run away from the Phoenix Indian School, and I didn't want to do that. Of course, I had run away from the Phoenix school before. I told Juan that I was not going to the Phoenix school. Juan asked, "Are you going to Santa Fe again?" "No," I said, "to the Albuquerque school." I told him that I was sorry to leave him after all he had done for me. He said, "Maybe you have a Navajo girl over there."

I was thankful that Mrs. White did not give me much for spending. Whenever I visited Phoenix with Juan María, I had a little money. Mrs. White asked me one day if I wanted her to send my wages to the superintendent at the Phoenix School for safekeeping. I begged her to give me the money and I would turn it in. I lied. I worked until the last week of September. I told Mrs. White that I was leaving and she was sorry to see me go. She asked me to come back again; then she gave me my money.

Juan and I went to Phoenix together and he stayed with me for several hours. I stayed in town for two days, and on the third day I decided to steal a ride on a freight train that night. I hung around near the depot out of sight. At midnight a train stopped for awhile, then started again. I ran and got on a tank car which had a catwalk all around it. I stood up all night watching for the brakeman, and every time the train stopped, I would get off and hide. The brakeman would walk along each side of the train with a stick in his hand. Toward daylight, the train was nearing a town. I jumped off—it was Tucson. From there I walked to town.

I had on a blue suit and cap, and they were dirty from the train ride. I was wearing two shirts so that I would not have to carry anything. I thought of my folks here in Tucson—I had not seen them for seven years. They had lived south of town when I had left for the Santa Fe school, and I did not know that they had recently moved to Chandler to work. I did not see my folks and I did not see anyone I knew, so I did not ask about them from any of the other Indians. I also walked by the Indian village near the Southern Pacific roundhouse because most of the people there were from near Comobabi. I knew those people, but I did not see my family. None of the Indians recognized me because I did not show my face.

I walked eastward along the railroad to where Park Avenue later crossed the tracks. Some hobos told me that it was hard to catch a train in Tucson because the police watched so closely. I waited most of the night. Some of the trains were going too fast, but toward morning one came which was not going too fast, and I caught it. I was on a tanker again. Before long it was getting light, and the train slowed down in some little place. I jumped down and hid in the bushes.

The next evening I caught another train; this time it was a boxcar. I stayed inside with some hobos. Early in the morning we came to a town — the hobos told me it was El Paso, Texas. I jumped off at the edge of town and walked in to get something to eat. I wandered around town for some time.

Again I waited for the night so I could catch a train. Outside of town I finally caught one — an empty coal car. When the train stopped in Las Cruces, a man climbed into the car and came over to where I was sitting. I was scared for awhile. When he said, "Hello," I felt better. He asked me where I was going. I told him that I was going back to the Indian school in Albuquerque. "Oh, you an Indian?" "Yes, a Papago from Tucson." We talked for awhile. He was eating, and he gave me some walnuts. He told me this car was not going ahead, and he pointed to the next train and told me to get on. He showed me his badge — he was an F.B.I. agent.

That night the train traveled fast. Fortunately, the night was not cold. I arrived in Albuquerque early in the morning and I got off before the train reached the main town. I walked in, as I always did, and then I hung around town for awhile before I walked to school. I remembered the school as having been two and a half miles north of town. I arrived at school during the afternoon. It was September, 1915. I asked a small boy who was playing on the lawn if he knew a student named Nero Talafa. He pointed to where I could find him. Nero was surprised to see me—and also glad.

Nero and I had both been on the Santa Fe team when we had defeated Albuquerque. He asked me if I wanted to go to school. I told him yes, if Mr. Perce would take me. Nero right away went to the superintendent's office and told him about me. "He is the boy who beat your team. He wants to enroll here if you will take him." Mr. Perce asked me if I had run away from some school. I lied and said, "No." He was glad to have me. I played baseball and football for them for two years, 1915 and 1916. I played against several high schools and the University of New Mexico.

I enjoyed those two years in Albuquerque and I was getting along just fine. I was now in the eighth grade. But Superintendent J.B. Brown at Phoenix found out that I was in the Albuquerque school because of stories in the school newspaper. It was in November 1916 when an office boy brought a note to my teacher. She read it, then looked toward where I was sitting, so I had a feeling that it must be something about me.

The teacher waited for awhile; then she called me to her desk and told me that I was to go to see the superintendent. Mr. Perce told me that I was wanted in Phoenix. He was very sorry to lose me. He said, "I'd like to keep you, but Superintendent Brown has asked that you be sent back." I told Mr. Perce that I did not want to go back there. For running away they would put me in confinement and whip me. Mr. Perce talked to Mr. Brown by long distance telephone. After that, he said, "I can do nothing; he has already sent tickets for you. Tomorrow you will take the train back to Phoenix." I went back to my class and told them that tomorrow I was going back to the Phoenix school. I told them that I was sorry to leave this school and this teacher. My class was just like a family, and there were many tears — mine also.

Next afternoon they took me to the depot and I waited for the train. I got on and rode all day. It reminded me of my longest walk from Rocky Ford to Phoenix. I thought, "I am now riding on a good train, on the same road." The train stopped in the same towns, including Flagstaff. When the train got into Phoenix, it was dark. As it slowed down, I thought about the punishment I would soon get at school. I almost jumped off, but something told me not to, so I stayed on.

When the train stopped, I did not get off right away. I was looking through the window and I saw Mr. Vane, the coach at school. He was walking along the cars looking for me. I liked the coach, and he had taught me much about baseball and football. When I stepped down, he was very glad to see me. He said, "Come back?" I said, "Yes." "We need you here at school."

He had a motorcycle and we rode to school. I was all dressed up in a greenish suit and sport cap. At the Phoenix school nobody—I mean the Indian boys—ever dressed in a suit. On our way, Mr. Vane said he was very glad that I was back to play on the team. I did not pay much attention to what he was saying half of the time. I was thinking, "What will happen tomorrow?" When we arrived at school, everyone was in bed. He showed me a bed to sleep in.

Next morning about 6:00 A.M. the buglers marched around the park blowing their call to get everyone up. It was just like the army—everybody hated to get up. On the second call, everybody lined up outside for roll call. I did not go out for the lineup because I didn't know where I belonged. The band played and they raised the flag. After that the students marched to the big mess hall for breakfast, and I followed them inside. Whenever a student did something wrong, they made him stand on a platform in front of the students. I stood alongside of our disciplinarian, Major Grestead. He had a bell in his hand and, when he rang it once, everyone sat down; with the second ring, they began to eat. The Phoenix school was very different from the Santa Fe and Albuquerque schools. It was like the army—very strict in everything.

I stood there for quite awhile; I thought that he would never place me. All of the students' eyes were on me; they remembered me. Finally the major found a place for me to sit. When the time was up, he rang the bell to stand up, and we marched out by companies to the parade ground for an hour of drill. The students were then dismissed—half to prepare for class, the others to go to their trades.

Later the major talked to me, then let me go. He sent me back to my old job on the farm. I always liked farm work. That year I planned to win the corn contest, and I had the best corn. But I left before the judging and another Papago boy, José Laria, took my corn to the contest and won first prize.

While I was at Phoenix, I worked at the East Farm, about four or five miles from the school and not far from the Montezuma Sanitarium. Once again I saw my former teacher from Santa Fe, Miss Fiston, who was now married to a farmer who worked for the Indian school. I was not at the Phoenix School very long before America got into World War I. That brought about an end to my school days.

The Army Years
1917 — 1922

America entered World War I in 1917. Before the war, the government did not want Indians to join the army; now they were urged to volunteer, but Indians were not drafted. Right away many of the boys at school volunteered in the Navy, Marines, Army, and National Guard. My friend, Webster Buffington, a Cherokee, and I tried to get in. First we tried the Army, but the recruiter turned us down. Then we tried the Navy and the Marines, but they said that we were too small—too short, too light. Webster and I were about the same size, 5 feet, 4 inches. He weighed 120, I was 125. We went back to school and told Superintendent Brown that everybody had turned us down—said that we were too small and couldn't do anything. He said, "I'll see about that," and he called somebody. Next day he said, "You go to the National Guard headquarters and they'll take you. You can protect our border."

We went to the National Guard and they signed us up. They fixed our papers and said to come back the next day. It was April 18, 1917, when we went back and signed all the papers. They shipped us right away to the little border town of Naco, Arizona. There we got our uniforms and some old Spanish-American War rifles.

When we got to Naco, Webster and I were surprised to find that there were many Indians in the Arizona 1st Infantry Regiment. Company F was all Indian, and I knew many of the boys there from our reservation and from school. Webster and I were put in Company A with two other Indian boys — Hudson Lockwood, a Cherokee, and Nolia, a Zuni from New Mexico. Nolia was a little fellow, smaller than me, and a cook.

We already knew how to drill with rifles from our training at school. After we got our uniforms we moved into big tents which held five men. They were surrounded by sandbags because of the bullets which came from over the border. The Mexicans were having a revolution, and their army was shooting at somebody. Most of the revolutionaries had gone, but some stayed and the shooting went on. The houses in Mexico had big holes in them and we could see trenches, and bodies lying around.

We had several regiments there at Naco to see that the Mexicans didn't come into the United States. There was the 7th Cavalry, a Regular-Army black unit, and National Guardsmen from Arizona, Colorado, New Mexico, and Wyoming. Our regiment was guarding a gate at the border. Our guard post was a tent surrounded by sandbags. We searched people who crossed into Arizona for firearms and other things. We searched everybody, and it was my first time to search a woman. I don't remember that we ever found anything.

I was in Naco several months and, one day, the officers told us to get ready to move out with full packs. Where we were going we did not know. In the army they don't tell you anything. So we pulled down our tents and everything was loaded on wagons. In those days we didn't know what a truck was. When everything was loaded, we started marching. Everybody was asking where we were going. It was late June or early July and a very hot day, but we didn't mind walking all day with heavy packs on our backs. I don't remember what time our company arrived at the little town of Lowell, which was near Bisbee. We put up our tents on a hill overlooking the village. Other companies went to Ajo, Globe, Miami, Jerome, and Bisbee.

We learned that all of the miners in Arizona were on strike. We called the strikers "Wobblies." Also at the mining towns were policemen and rangers on horseback. The soldiers and policemen drove the strikers from their homes. The big drive started at Bisbee and went through the canyon toward Lowell. The National Guardsmen spread through Bisbee and looked in every home for strikers. Women were crying because of their husbands. Some of the miners tried to escape over the hills. They looked, from a distance, like ants trying to run away. The rangers chased them on horseback.

The miners were rounded up and marched to a ball park on the other side of a little settlement called

Warren. There were about fifteen hundred of them. On the same day, a train brought a lot of cattle cars. The policemen marched the miners inside the cattle cars and armed guards got on top of the cars. The miners were dumped somewhere in New Mexico.

After the strikers were gone, I heard men talking about the Bisbee dance halls, saloons, and bad cowboys. We were not permitted to visit those places, but I thought about going over there to see them for myself. That night I "snaked" out of camp when I thought everybody was asleep. I had civilian clothes hidden behind some rocks; I changed out of my uniform and walked into Bisbee.

I was kind of afraid that some of the officers from camp might see me. If they caught me in Bisbee, I'd be put in the guardhouse. The streets were dark, not lighted like now. I saw many people walking in front of saloons. From across the street I could see in the bars where there were women in short skirts like you see in the movies. A drunk man was thrown out of one bar. I hung around watching all of this for some time, then I decided to go home.

I reached our camp, changed into my uniform, and again "snaked" into the tent. Nobody seemed to have noticed me and I was soon in bed—it was almost morning. I didn't tell anybody until many months afterward.

We were in Lowell over a week when our captain got word that we were to return to Naco. We broke camp, loaded the wagons again with our tents and things, and shouldered full packs. We had our things rolled inside our blankets, which went over the right shoulder. The whole thing looked like a donut. The

71

march was hot. The companies at other mining towns were farther away and they had not shown up when we reached Naco, but in a few days the regiment was reassembled.

Rumors said that we were about to leave, and everybody tried to guess where. Soon our captain gave us the news that we were going to Camp Kearney, California, near La Jolla. Everybody was happy, for many of us had never been to California and we were anxious to see what it looked like. Finally the time came for us to pull down our tents again. This time we loaded them on a train; then the men loaded in cars and left Naco. The sun was down when the train left, and we did not know in what direction we were going.

Somewhere between midnight and 2:00 A.M., the train stopped and we were in Tucson. People in town knew that our train was coming and my parents had come and waited for a long time. I was one of the platform guards, and I soon saw my brother José and the government matron for Indian girls, Mrs. Woodruff. They looked for me and found me on duty behind the trees on Congress Street. They told me that Mother and Father had gotten tired and left.

The people who came to see their boys brought us coffee and sandwiches. After an hour the train was ready to go and we guards had to get on. I said good-bye to José and Mrs. Woodruff. (While I was overseas in France, Mrs. Woodruff wrote letters to me for my parents. She is the one who gave me my name of James.)

In California we arrived at Camp Kearney. I believe that our regiment was the first to arrive, and the camp was just being built. I saw men leveling the ground with tractors. The powdery dirt was soft and we sank into it almost to our knees. We walked to the other end of the clearing, which was where we were to put up our tents. We had little cots to sleep on but we had to water the ground to keep down the dust. In time the ground seemed to harden and walking was easier. Other units arrived daily and tents and frame buildings went up everywhere.

Once our unit had its tents up, we began to drill every day but Saturday and Sunday. Soon our unit got draftees to fill up our company to 250 men. We drilled hard and eventually were involved in division maneuvers. One day, not long after we arrived, a sergeant told me, "You're going to be on kitchen police." I thought that he meant that I was going to be a policeman—I thought I was going to wear a star. A friend of mine said, "He didn't mean policeman. You're going to wash dishes there—and lots of pots and pans." He was right.

After the maneuvers, we had time for some recreation. I got several passes and went to San Diego. Even though our camp was only five miles from the beach, I didn't get to go until one day we were marched over for a swim. We undressed and left our uniforms on the sand. After a while, a storm came up and we were told to leave the water. Some good swimmers had gone far out and did not hear the alarm. When we dressed, their uniforms were still on the beach. Our men looked for them but they were lost. I never learned how many drowned.

I had sinus trouble and went to the hospital in April 1918, but I was soon on duty again. Early in

June, a sergeant asked for volunteers to go overseas. Right away, I volunteered. Some of the men thought I was foolish and said, "They're going to kill you over there." When I told my Indian friends that I had volunteered, Webster Buffington and Hudson Lockwood joined me and we went together. The volunteers were told to clean up and we passed in review before the generals. Somebody took a picture and I bought one to send to my folks in Arizona.

We traveled east in Pullman cars. We rode for several days and stopped in Kansas City and Chicago. On our way, many people stood along the railroad watching the troop train. They handed out many things to men — cakes, donuts, sweet bread, and such. Sometimes the train was going too fast, so the people would put a wire loop on their food packages, and the boys would hold out their arms and catch them, like they used to do with train orders.

We arrived at Camp Dix, which was big, but not like Camp Kearney. It was a permanent camp with two-story, frame barracks. It was our embarkation center and we did not stay there very long. While we were at Camp Dix, they let us go on pass to New York City and other towns. In camp I made friends with an Italian boy who had relatives in Newark, New Jersey. He wanted to take me to meet them because they had never seen an Arizona Indian. They had lived all their lives in New Jersey and had not visited other states. They were nice people and they asked me what I would like to eat — and if I had ever tried spaghetti. I told them that I hadn't, so they cooked some for me. I tried to pick it up with my fork, but it slipped off.

They laughed and showed me how to roll it before picking it up. I had a lot of fun with that.

Twice the boy took me to visit New York City. It was a big town and I did not like the noise. I had never seen tall buildings like those—it made me dizzy just looking up at them. I knew that if I were by myself I would get lost. We rode on some street cars and the subway. We came up somewhere but, since the boy lived in the area, he knew his way around. The second time that we went to New York, the Italian boy left me in a park near the Singer Building while he went to see somebody. Time passed and I thought that he'd never come back. I was worried. I didn't know how to get back to camp.

One day we were notified to get our things together and be ready to move out at any moment. That night we carried our packs and marched from Camp Dix to the river. There was a barge waiting for us to load on. It took us to a ship which already had some soldiers aboard. We stayed in New York harbor for two or three days, but we could not leave the ship. The ship sailed one night. I thought that we were the only ship going, but two days out we woke up to see lots of ships all around—big ones, little ones—maybe sixty or eighty of them. There were destroyers around the convoy and a big battleship in front. We knew then that a lot of men were going over.

The first morning many of the boys were seasick and didn't want to eat anything. They lay around on the deck. I didn't get seasick, but the food didn't taste right, so I didn't eat it. I was really thankful for one old sergeant at Camp Dix. He had been to the

Philippines and Panama, and he told me to take along apples, oranges, or lemon drops to eat on the trip. He said that it would help and I wouldn't get seasick. I had plenty of lemon drops and apples, and they helped, just like the sergeant said.

Every day I would go up on deck and stand on the bow of the ship while it went up and down like a rocker. I enjoyed it. I didn't count the days of the trip, but it was a long time before I saw land. When I did, somebody said it was England. The ship landed at Liverpool. It was cloudy, foggy, and rainy, so I couldn't see anything.

As soon as the ship docked, we were told to get off in the rain and we began to march. We marched quite a way from the port to reach an English army camp. Their tents were smaller than the American tents and they were round, with ten men in each tent. Our tent was not good: it had many holes in it and leaked all over. There were no cots, so we all lay on the ground with our feet sticking outside. It rained all night and nobody undressed. I couldn't sleep.

It appeared that we were going to stay at this camp for awhile, so our commander let us walk out in the country, but we could not visit the cities. I was interested in the English homes with the grass roofs which did not leak. When it was not raining, we would walk about and talk to the farmers. I could not understand them very well—they talked too fast for me.

A friend and I visited a family. After they learned that I was an Indian from Arizona, they asked me many questions. They wanted to know if, at home, I wore feathers and painted my face. I told them that Indians had a new life and were the same as other people. Some went to school, built homes, and were getting civilized—but many were poor. My people worked for the white men everywhere. They seemed interested to hear me talk. One man said, "You must have a good education." I said that I only had an elementary education and that learning English was hard at first. These people asked us to come back before going to France, but I did not see them again.

After a few days, our 1st Sergeant told us that we were leaving soon so we should not leave camp. We kept our things ready. One foggy, rainy, wet morning we packed. When the time came, we marched in the rain past London and onward until we reached Dover on the English Channel. There we were loaded on a cattle boat that would take us to Le Havre, France. The boat was filthy, with fresh cow manure so deep on the deck that none of us would lie down. We had to stand all night.

In the morning we got off and marched across the railroad yard to load onto a train. Our car was so crowded that many men could not sit down and had to stand, as they had all night. At least the cars were clean. I was lucky, for I got a seat in the doorway with my legs hanging down. Many men slept, regardless of the crowding.

The train was slow. In one rail yard where we stopped, we could get off the train. There were lots of cars on each side of us and the men spread out looking them over. Pretty soon some of our men came back rolling a barrel of wine. They got to our car with it and lifted it up, then smashed in the top. Oh boy, did those guys drink! Some of them said, "Come on, Chief (they always called me "Chief"). Come on and get some." They took the wine with their canteen cups, and pretty soon a lot of them were drunk and lying on top of one another. I didn't drink any. We stayed there several hours; then we went on. I still had my seat in the door.

The train took us near the Marne River and unloaded us at Chateau-Thierry. From there we marched across the river and toward the Belleau Woods. It was about three o'clock in the morning, but they divided us into groups, and Webster Buffington and Hudson Lockwood and I were assigned to Company D, 109th Infantry Regiment, 28th Infantry Division. The 109th was originally from Pennsylvania. When we got to Company D we found that it was very short of men, as were most of the companies in the regiment after their recent fight in the Second Battle of the Marne.

More than ever, we Indian boys stuck together. As soon as we arrived, our company began to move. That night was rainy, and the ground was very muddy. We could not walk very fast, for it was too slippery. Men often fell down in the mud. There were German dead everywhere, and in the dark it scared me to step on a dead one. That mud was deep and soft and it was a black night in that forest. All of us new boys were scared.

When it was daylight, we came out in the open. Ahead was a wheat field and I saw many men way out in front. The wheat was so tall that I could just see the men's heads. This was the first time that we new boys were under artillery fire. When it came, everybody fell to the ground. The shells were falling all around us and we were scared. I don't know if anyone was hit but I remember that shells came very close to me. I lay flat on my stomach. As soon as the firing began, one of the new boys was rolling on the ground and crying. It was just as if he had been hit. The sergeant looked at him. I was lying on one side of him and I tried to hold him down. They said that he was shell-shocked. They took him away, I guess, for I never saw him again.

Later, we were ordered to move on. When we came to the top of a hill, I could see many men lining up in a crooked line. They were moving toward the German position, and the enemy machine guns cut them down like wheat—hundreds of them. I could see them from a distance. We were going pretty slow. We would move a short distance, then rest a bit, then start again. When we got down in a valley, we found lots of holes—I guess the Germans dug them. We got in them and our commander said to stay there. "Don't come out. Stay down." When I looked up at the hill, there were American soldiers all over. Some of those boys had tried to dig in with their knives, but they got killed. There were hundreds of men killed right there.

We were there maybe half a day. Everybody was hungry—seems like I hadn't eaten much for three days. We took rations from the dead men's packs and ate those. We were also thirsty, but all the canteens were empty. The sergeant said that somebody would have to go after water from a little stream that we could see several hundred yards away. Nobody wanted to go. So he said, "What about you, Chief? Can you get over there?" There were lots of guys thirsty and I made up my mind to go. So I told the sergeant, "All right, I'll go." Another Arizona boy, a white boy, said he'd go along. As the sun went down, we "snaked" along some low ground like I did at Bisbee, and we got to the stream. The little river was bloody and later we saw some dead Germans in the stream. We had a lot of canteens and we filled them up. We crawled back the way we came and got to the company all right. I was sure scared but the boys were happy to get a little water.

After sundown, our company relieved some company of the 32nd Division. We stayed in some foxholes until early morning; then we crawled toward the wooded hill ahead. Somebody had circled around and killed the German machine gunners, so we all went up the hill and took it. The Germans were on the other side of the hill and there was a path through the woods. One of my Arizona friends was a sergeant who had been stationed at Naco. He was standing in the open looking through his field glasses when a German sniper shot him between the eyes. This was the first one of us new men to be killed that I know of.

Our company commander was a lieutenant—I never knew his name. He gave me a French Chauchat automatic rifle which had clips that were moonshaped. I think that there were thirty rounds in a clip and I had six clips in a bag. It seemed kind of heavy and I didn't think I was strong enough to carry it. They said, "You'll handle it." They showed me how to fire it and I got to where I liked it.

Once I remember that we were lying on the edge of some woods. Germans were hiding behind bushes and trees like we were. When they came out, they ran to their machine gun emplacement about two hundred yards away. We started shooting and I got one man. A second one ran and then turned and rolled on the ground. I guess I hit him, too, for he lay still. "Pretty good shooting, Chief," the boys called.

During the night the Germans left, so we got out of the woods and walked toward the Vesle River. There was a town of Fismes, deep in the valley along the Vesle River. Some of our men were fighting in the town; others of us were on the hills, but getting lots of artillery. They had us on guard on a high bank overlooking Fismes Valley, with two men to a foxhole. There were so many holes here that it was like a big cheese — we called it Limburger cheese.

We had a lot of machine guns, and the American artillery, pulled by big mules, set up not far behind us. One day German artillery fired on us most of the day. It killed the artillery mules and knocked out our kitchen, so we didn't get any food for three or four days. I weighed about 135 pounds when I joined the 109th, but I was now so thin that I used up my last belt hole and I could hardly keep my pants up.

They kept shelling us during the night. I was on the outpost with a machine gun when it began. Those big shells hit on our side and went, "BBWRECK!" They didn't sound like other shells — I guess they were mortars. I saw smoke coming from where the shells hit — just sort of curling up slow. At Camp Dix they had shown us about gas, but we thought that someone would always yell, "Gas" and sound an alarm when it was coming our way. I smelled something, but it wasn't like the stuff at Camp Dix and I didn't put my mask on. Besides, I had a different kind of mask than we'd had back there. When I began to smell the gas pretty strong, I put the mask on and I had it on for a long time. After awhile I couldn't stand it anymore and I took the mask off.

Most of the men in my company were gassed, and they were just lying around, lazy and sleeping. When I came off outpost the next day, I lay down under a tree just like the others. I felt lazy and kind of weak, like I was going to sleep. I had blisters on my skin, but I didn't even look at those. The sergeant came over: "Wake up, Chief. Gonna sleep all day?" Then he saw how I looked—my skin and all. "You're gassed," he said, and he called to another man to take me to the first-aid station. Two men carried me there on a stretcher, but, while I was waiting for the ambulance, I decided to go back to the company. The sergeant saw me and had another stretcher take me back to the first-aid station, and they tied me down so that I couldn't get off.

I was taken to a field hospital and there the doctor looked at me. I didn't cough very much but my face was blistered and all green. I was in the hospital about a week, I guess. Each day they put me into a tub of white stuff which looked like white lime. It cut down on the burning.

A priest came to see me at the hospital and talked to me about my folks back home. At this time I didn't know where my parents were living, but he wanted to write them for me. He asked my father's name and I told him. I guess that he got the name wrong, for he sent the letter to the San Xavier Mission and my father never got it. They sent it back to France. After awhile Mrs. Woodruff, the government matron back home, got the information and told my folks that I was in the hospital.

One day I begged the priest to help get me out. He said that I was still sick. "You stay a little longer," he said. I was lonesome for my company and my Indian friends, and I was feeling a little better, so one morning before breakfast I got up and walked out. Nobody paid much attention to me. I still had on my pajamas — no shoes, no hat. It was early in the morning as I walked toward the front lines, and nobody was on the road yet. I came to a little village and I saw an M.P. I tried to hide, but he saw me. He waved his arm for me to stop and he asked me where I was heading. I told him that I was going to Company D, 109th Infantry. He asked, "In those clothes?" The M.P. called the hospital and they came for me. I guess they thought I was a nut.

By the time that I got out of the hospital, the 109th had moved up near the Argonne Forest. I learned that my friend, Webster Buffington, had been shot in the mouth. I thought that he was killed and he was always in my mind. We had been together in school, in Naco, Bisbee, Camp Kearney, and then in France. After the war I learned that they had sent him to a hospital, then to Phoenix, and then he went back to live in Oklahoma.

I remember a lot of the fighting and also lots of things which now seem sort of funny. In the Argonne Forest I had trouble with my stomach — diarrhea. We were in trenches and I couldn't always get to the straddle trench because there were so many men. One time I got out of the trench where there were a lot of trees. I told a friend that I just had to "go." I got on top of a dirt pile and pulled my pants down. Everybody said, "Come on down here. They'll shoot you." I couldn't stand the diarrhea and I stayed up. The Germans shot at me but they missed. After awhile I crawled down into the trench again but I still had the cramps. I still had diarrhea when one day I was ordered to go on patrol. Food had just arrived after several days when we didn't have any. I got my first bite when a private told me that I was to go with him. I put the food down and I figured to get it later.

The private had never been on a patrol before and he was wearing a slicker raincoat; I had on an overcoat. Every time he took a step that raincoat made a noise. I told him that the slicker made too much noise, but he didn't pay any attention to me. We moved slow. It was dark and cold, and I had a feeling that something was going to happen. Suddenly a grenade was thrown at us from a hole somewhere. It was so dark that I didn't know it was a "potato masher." The private was on my right and he was closer to the explosion. He went down and I knew that he was hit. I also went down and I could feel a pain in my side.

Some Germans came running toward us. They looked at the private and knew he was dead. One came to me and picked me up. I felt the pain and I was limping. I walked very slowly. We moved away from our lines and, when it was daylight, we came to a farm house. I guess it wasn't very far back. I felt sick from my diarrhea, the pain in my side, and from having been gassed a second time.

In that farmhouse were prisoners—both Americans and French. A big American sergeant met us. I told him that I was sick with diarrhea and that I'd better stay outside. They put me in what looked like a woodshed and I stayed there. It was cold and I just had my overcoat. I could see from the hole in the overcoat where I had been hit. I told the sergeant how I felt, and he said they'd fix me up when we got to a prisoner camp. He thought that it would be soon.

The sergeant told me that I had been outside two days when they marched us to where there was a train that took us to a prison camp. The prison camp was about half a mile from Rastatt, Germany. Some men could hardly walk and it was slow going. All of the old prisoners came out to help us. They carried me to the bath house, clipped my hair, gave me a shower and clean clothes. Then I got a good meal — the first in days. There were lots of prisoners there — Americans, British, and French. Some had been there a long time. The Red Cross gave us a box with everything in it — clothes and canned goods. It seems like I got mine two times.

I was not in this camp very long, for after a week they sent some of us out to work in a sugar mill. Most of the men were assigned to shovel beets into a grinder at night. The boss was a good man and spoke good English. He saw that I was weak, so he gave me a job upstairs where it was warm and I only had to shovel back the ground-up beets which had fallen out of the trough.

Some of the prisoners made trouble. About a week after we started work, somebody threw an iron plate in with the beets and it broke something in the machine and it stopped. German soldiers asked who did it and nobody told. When they hit some of the men, the men tried to escape over the wire fence. The soldiers chased them and one colored man got stuck in the behind with a bayonet. He hollered and hollered. All the men were caught and, right away, they marched us inside and locked us up. There was no more work and we were sent back to the prison camp at Rastatt.

Soon afterward, the war was over. I was still in the prison camp and I still limped a little. One day another prisoner told me he would like to go to town to see somebody. He asked me, "How would you like to go to town?" I asked him how we could get out of the camp, and he said he would think of something. I thought about it a little while; then I said, "I'll go." There were two barbed-wire fences around the camp. I wrapped some old clothes around the wire and, as I was the smallest, I worked my way through. The other boy followed. The guards didn't see us and we took a path through the brush to the town.

There were crowds of German soldiers drinking, and the officers were with women. They saw us but paid no attention. The boy spoke good German and he talked to some of the women. They asked him who I was. When he told them that I was an American Indian, everybody touched my face. We went from one place to another until daylight and then walked back to camp.

The guard was surprised when we went to the gate, and he asked us how we had gotten out. The camp was quiet and the barracks were a mess. Every bunk was broken and there were blankets all over the place. I had had some souvenirs in a box which I wanted to take home. The box was broken and they were gone. The guard told us that during the night the prisoners were put on a train and taken back to France. The guard said, "You guys will have to wait until others come to take you."

After two days a guard told us to get ready to go to town to take a train to Switzerland. The train stopped near a lake at Basle, and the Red Cross gave us everything we needed and some little Red Cross flags. Then I was sent to a hospital in Vichy, France. After a check-up at the hospital, I was returned to Company D, 109th, which was then south of Toul. We had to do a lot of training and we spent a lot of time in athletics. Our commander called the men together one day and asked for volunteers to be in the occupation army on the Rhine. Well, this time I didn't volunteer. I wanted to go home.

In the middle of March 1919, our division was moved to Le Mans and we got ready to go home. We were given new uniforms, had group pictures taken, and put on a big parade for General Pershing. A month later we took a train for St. Nazaire and loaded on board the *Maui*. This time it did not take so long to cross the Atlantic. I think that we landed at Hoboken, although our division history says it was Philadelphia. We went to Camp Dix. The Pennsylvania boys were kept there for a big parade in Philadelphia, but the rest of us were discharged right away. My discharge was on May 8, 1919, but I signed up the same day for three more years in the Regular Army.

While we were coming home, I hadn't thought about reenlisting, but I made up my mind that I wanted to go someplace. I thought maybe I'd go to Panama, but the recruiting sergeant said, "Don't go

there. Too many mosquitos. They're as big as flies."
So I decided to go to China or the Philippines. As
soon as I had signed my reenlistment papers, I took a
month's leave and went to Arizona. Mother was living at the San Xavier Reservation, but my father was
away working and I didn't get to see him. There was
no ceremony when I came back home. Most of the
time I stayed in my uniform. After a time I went to
visit friends in Phoenix; then I stopped for awhile in
Chicago. From there I returned to Camp Dix. Soon
they had a group of recruits ready and we were sent
by train to San Francisco.

At first I was at the Presidio; later I was sent to
Angel Island Barracks, where I stayed for a month
while waiting for the transport. Our ship was the
John A. Logan, and we had a lot of men aboard going
to different places. We left San Francisco in the
daytime and passed through the Golden Gate. Once
we were at sea, it got a bit rough and some of the men
got seasick right away. I didn't mind the weather
because I had been across the Atlantic and I knew
how to take care of myself.

It took over a week to reach Honolulu and we
stayed there several days. We were given passes so that
we could look over the city and countryside. I was
especially interested in seeing the pineapple planta-
tions and the growing of sugar cane. The ship took on
coal in Honolulu and we left for Guam. It took longer
than going to Honolulu and the weather was hot. In
port they stretched canvas over the deck to keep off
the sun. The ship unloaded some sailors and cargo in
the two days that we were there.

Our next stop was in Manila. As we crossed the ocean, one day it was Sunday, and the next day it was also Sunday. When we reached the Philippine Islands, we passed through a number of islands. We stopped quite awhile in Manila and all the passengers unloaded and went to Fort McKinley. We had passes to visit the city and the countryside. The country was pretty—everything was green everywhere. We even saw bananas growing wild on the mountains.

Our next stop was in Nagasaki, Japan, where we stayed for a week or ten days. The ship was loaded with coal by Japanese women. The women carried big baskets of coal on their heads and dumped the coal in the ship's bin. The women lined up like ants and made a continuous line all day long. It was a sight to watch the women work like men.

Our commander wouldn't let the men off the ship, but rowboats came alongside and offered things for sale. Some of the soldiers wanted to get off pretty bad. In the night they climbed down a rope to some of those rowboats and went ashore. A soldier asked me to go with him but I said, "No, I'll stay on the ship." I was afraid that I might get caught and I didn't want to have a bad record in the army. The next morning the sergeant was checking around the ship to see if everyone was aboard. He found very few men on the ship. Right away he sent the M.P.s to round up the boys in town. The M.P.s brought the men back and they were confined on the ship. Meanwhile, the sergeant made a list of the men who had not jumped ship and the next day he gave us each a twenty-four-hour pass. I went to town with a group of friends.

Some of the boys wanted to get tattoos on their arms and chests. One boy got a big tattoo on his chest. Then he said, "Why don't you put something on your arm?" I didn't want it because I knew that it would hurt, for I already had a tattoo on my left arm that I had got in Colorado. He said, "No, it won't hurt," and he told the Japanese man to put a Japanese woman on my arm. They wanted her to be undressed, but I didn't want that. They put on the tattoo — and it sure hurt a lot.

While we were in Nagasaki, I looked at many stores, but it was hard to make the people understand what we wanted to buy. I didn't eat or drink anything, and I went back on board ship that night. I went ashore twice more while we were in port. When we left Nagasaki it was daytime, and the ocean looked yellow. I guess that's why it's called the Yellow Sea. Most of us didn't know where our next stop would be. It was Vladivostok, in Siberia, where the 30th Infantry Regiment was stationed. We left some men there and we took others aboard who were going home. From there we went on to China.

The ship anchored at Chin Wang Tao. It wasn't a town, just a series of warehouses for the Army. We got off the ship and waited several hours for the train which was to take us to Tientsin and the 15th Infantry Regiment. We watched the ship unload cargo for our regiment and for the Marines in Peking. They told me that it was eighty or ninety miles from the port to Tientsin. We rode the train in passenger cars, and I looked at the country, which was like the Arizona desert. When we arrived in Tientsin, there was a guide to show us to our barracks. We walked about two miles to the 15th Infantry compound. It looked very nice, with many two-storied buildings of red brick.

I was assigned to Company D, 15th Infantry—a machine gun company. The first thing we did was to clean up and look around. They issued us three kinds of uniforms and other equipment. We had to stay inside the compound for a few days until everything was straightened out. After a few days, they let us go see the city. The U.S. Army barracks was located in the southwest part of the city, almost on the edge. Tientsin was a very large city; the Hai River ran through it, and big ships would come up the river from the sea. Later I learned that the English, French, Portuguese, Italians, Russians, and Japanese also had troops stationed in the city.

It was pretty easy living for us Americans. Each soldier had Chinese boys to do his cleaning, shine his shoes, fix his bed, clean his clothes, and do everything. The price was one American dollar a month. I found Chinese boys to do all of my work for me. I liked them and I gave them extra pay when they did a good job. One dollar was a lot of money for the Chinese.

Every payday I got thirty dollars, which was paid in gold—a ten-dollar and a twenty-dollar gold coin. I had the paymaster hold back twenty-five dollars for me, and I kept only five dollars. I never spent my five dollars before the end of the month—I always had money left over. I didn't gamble, and I didn't lend money to other men.

I liked my new home, and I didn't get homesick. Then in 1920 I got my first letter from home—it was sent by Mrs. Woodruff. She told me that my family had been in an auto accident near Tucson. My brother, José, was driving his Dodge from Coolidge to Tucson when it went out of control on a hill. My mother, father, and brother were injured and taken to St. Mary's Hospital. My father died two days later; my mother lived, but she was hurt bad. The letter was three months old when I got it and I was too far away to go and see my family. I answered Mrs. Woodruff's letter, and then I tried to forget about the accident.

The winters in China were very cold, with much rain and snow. We had to wear our big, long overcoats and heavy caps with ear flaps. In January 1921, I fell while ice skating and broke my nose; I had to go to the hospital to have it fixed. Summers were very nice in Tientsin. Sometimes we hired a rickshaw for sight-seeing. There were hundreds of rickshaws every-where. Many of them waited right in front of our compound ready to take soldiers out for a ride. It only cost a dime to go anyplace.

Once a friend asked me to go with him to see the Chinese executions on the north side of town, about twelve miles away. This boy had been in Tientsin for some time and he knew the way. The killings were done in a big graveyard about a mile long and half a mile wide. I was surprised to find that there were many American soldiers there to watch. "We are just in time," he said. There was a parade of men carrying signs saying that these prisoners would be executed.

That day the Chinese killed forty-five men. They

brought them forward one at a time and a policeman shot them in the head with a pistol. There was a trench about forty or fifty feet long and six feet deep. Every time one was shot, men would throw his body in the pit. They let us get close to the shooting. I had a little camera with me and I still have some pictures of the shootings. After a while, I could not stand to watch it anymore. I told my friend, and we left for home. I did not go again, but some of the soldiers would watch every time there were executions.

I was in a machine-gun company, and we trained hard. Our gun was carried in a little cart pulled by a mule. My job was to lead the mule, and I trained her good. I had worked with mules at the Indian school in Santa Fe and I knew how to treat them. Anyway, I taught the mule to start quick, turn, and stop. I guess that's why they picked me and the mule to take part in a sports event in the Philippine Islands during the summer of 1920. I was surprised when I learned of our selection.

Later that summer one squad of Company D boarded the train at Tientsin depot. At Chin Wang Tao we boarded a ship for Manila. Every man in the squad knew Fort McKinley and we were pleased to be visiting there. The Army had a great fair. One night we saw fireworks, and during the next day we saw many things. That evening our captain explained to us what we were going to do the next day.

When the contest began, six machine-gun carts were lined up in a row. Some belonged to the 9th Cavalry (Colored), 1st Philippine Infantry, and other units. At a signal, we ran fifty yards, turned around, loaded the gun, positioned it, fired six to ten rounds, dismantled the gun, loaded it in the cart, and ran back to the starting line. In this contest, one of the Philippine gunners forgot to block his gun; when he fired, the gun jumped back and knocked out his front teeth. The next contest was to climb a ten-foot wall while carrying the gun and then put it into action. In the several events, our squad won.

After the contests we spent about ten days sightseeing while waiting for a boat to take us back to China. Our boys went crazy over the bananas, which grew everywhere, and the coconuts and other fruit. When it came time to leave, we were sorry to go. Everyone wanted to do more sightseeing and have a good time.

Back in China, we continued training. I also worked in the bakery, making bread, and sometimes I was an M.P. Best of all were the sports. I played basketball and baseball on the company teams. We had no football team, but we played push ball. The ball was eight feet high and company teams tried to out-push one another. I also did some boxing.

In Company D, a seven-year-old boy named Spud was our mascot. Spud had been abandoned and left to die when he was very small. Some of the soldiers took care of him. He always wore a U.S. Army uniform, and he spoke good English. I didn't go out very much, but in June 1921 I decided to see Peking. My company commander gave me a week's leave and I took Spud with me as an interpreter. When I told him that we were going to Peking, he was very happy.

I had my things put away before I left, and I did not take much with me. The train trip to Peking was about seventy miles. When we arrived, I told Spud that we would look for a hotel. Spud asked a Chinaman, and he pointed to a tall building. The hotel was seven stories tall and was very nice inside. I don't know how much I paid for the six nights, but it wasn't much—everything was very cheap in China. Our room was on the fifth floor.

All of the hotel porters were dressed in white, and some spoke English. The porters told us where to go to see things.

The first afternoon we walked around near the hotel looking at things. I took lots of pictures. Everywhere we went, the Chinese people kept looking at me. Spud said that the people asked him what kind of a person I was. Spud asked me, for he wanted to be able to tell them. I said, "Tell them that I am an American Indian." People looked at me and they often wanted to touch me.

We saw much of Peking and the small towns nearby. We went for several camel rides. On my first the rocking back and forth almost made me seasick. Then we got a permit to visit the Forbidden City because I had heard so much about it. A secret policeman was with us all the time to watch us. Everything inside was marble and looked nice. I was very interested in the Chinese gods, or Buddhas. A guard took a picture of Spud and me coming out of the palace.

Another great event was going up on the Great Wall near the West Gate. There was a guard on the wall. Spud talked to the guard and asked him to have his picture taken with me. He said, "Din-How." I took the guard's rifle and pointed it at him while Spud took a picture. We had a great time in Peking and we were sorry to have to leave. We told the porters good-bye and they were sorry to see us go. I took pictures of them and I had my picture taken with them. Soon I was to leave China. All these years, however, I have wondered what happened to Spud. I still think of him.

Not long after I returned from Peking, our battalion was transferred to the Philippine Islands. Everyone was surprised, and many of the boys didn't want to go. They had been in China for a long time, and some of them had families. One of my friends in the bakery had a pretty Japanese wife and four daughters. Other soldiers had married Chinese or Korean girls.

We took a transport to Manila, and we were marched to Fort McKinley. We stayed about two weeks, then marched to the river to load on a small boat which took us to Camp Eldridge, near Los Baños, which was about fifty miles east of Manila and fairly high. It was a very pretty place, always green, with fruit trees everywhere. Nearly all of the Filipinos made their homes of bamboo with grass roofs. The jungle was all around. Unlike China, it was always green, always warm. At first the boys couldn't get enough fruit. They ate pineapples, papayas, coconuts, and bananas like monkeys. I was the same way. After awhile we got tired of the fruit and slowed down.

Our camp was located near a lake and there was a hot spring nearby. The water was so hot that you could cook a chicken by just putting it in the water. The Army had a house there for steam baths, and I enjoyed them. It cost nothing.

I was in the Philippines almost a year. As in China, we did little fatigue duty or personal work, for we hired Filipino boys to do it. In China I had often been on M.P. duty. In the Philippines this was what I did most of the time. We had lots of time for athletics, so we organized a baseball team. Pvt. Canfield was our pitcher, and I played shortstop. One of our officers was our manager, and he got us games with other military teams. Each Saturday and Sunday we played Philippine teams. Those Filipino boys loved to play baseball.

The Philippine Agricultural University was in town, and I met many of the students. My student friends often invited me for dinner. They were very good people, and being with them was almost like being with my own people. They were very sorry when it was time for me to go back to the United States, and they gave me a farewell party. I had thought many times about whether to reenlist or go home. My friends wanted me to stay. I liked the Army in China and the Philippines, but I still made up my mind to get out.

One day they called out the names of the men going back to the States, and I was one of them. We took the same small boat back to Manila. Many people turned out to see me and to say goodbye. When we got to Manila, our transport, the *Sherman*, was waiting for us and we went aboard. I thought that we were the only ones, but soldiers came from other camps. There were sailors going home, too. The next day the ship started, and the trip took about three weeks. We stopped in Honolulu, but not for very long. It was a lonesome trip, a long ride.

When we arrived in San Francisco, I was transferred to the Presidio and assigned to Company A, 19th Infantry. While in California, our unit went across the Golden Gate in a small boat to Fort Baker. We stayed there for about a month, mostly doing target practice. We had no place to go because there was no town near, so I just stayed in camp. After the target practice, we returned to the Presidio. I was then given my discharge on July 22, 1922.

Seeing the Country
1922 – 1929

When I left the army, I was undecided what to do—go home or look around. I decided to stay in California for awhile. I had a little back pay and the several hundred dollars which the paymaster had held for me. While in San Francisco, I visited many places I had not seen before. I always liked to see new things.

One day I decided to visit Sacramento, for other boys had talked about going there when they got out of the Army. I asked a man about going by boat. "It's cheap but slow going," he said. I believe that I paid three dollars one way. The boat traveled all night and arrived after the sun was up. I got off and set out to see the town. I hung around there for two weeks, but I did not try to find a job.

One night I heard a man talking about gambling in the houseboats along the river. I decided to see this, but the man told me not to go by myself, for there were many bad people around there. I went anyway. It was midnight, and nobody noticed me. I just looked on. There was much gambling and many drunks.

I did not know anybody around Sacramento, but one day I met an Indian. He asked me if I lived there. I told him that I had just gotten out of the Army and was visiting. He said that he came from a reservation just south of town, but that he was working picking hops at the little town of Ione. I didn't know what hops were. He described them and told me about picking. He was the boss of the pickers, and he asked me if I'd like to try. I agreed.

The Indian had a little Ford with no top in which we rode about twelve miles south of town to the camp. There were many pickers camped there. This man was a family man; he had a big family, all living in tents. There was one extra tent, and I slept in it. He asked me to eat with his family until I bought some cooking things and got settled. They were very nice people. Next day I tried picking hops. Each person got a big basket, about twenty-gallon size, and received twenty-five cents for each basketful. I was not very fast at first, but I soon learned.

We didn't work on Sundays. The pickers had a baseball team and a ball field. The boss-man played ball; he was forty-six years old, but fast. I watched them practice every evening after work. I just loved baseball and football, and I carried my glove and shoes everywhere in my suitcase. The boys didn't know that I played—I guess I didn't look like I played anything. They never asked me. One evening the boss was throwing the ball to his son-in-law in front of his tent. He missed one, so I picked it up and threw it back to him. Right away he asked me if I played ball, and I said, "A little." He asked me to come to the ball ground. He soon saw that I could play ball, and he put me on third base.

Next Sunday we played a team from some little town and we beat them. From that time on, everybody thought I was a good player. Then we played a team in Sacramento. The boys played good ball. They were surprised when they found out that I was from Arizona. They didn't know that we played baseball in Arizona—they thought all Arizonians were cowboys!

About that time, the Indians were having a big powwow on the nearby reservation. There was a carnival and many other things going on—Indian dancing, men playing football against a girl's team, baseball, and gambling. I walked around all that night because I had no place to sleep. In the morning we rode back to camp and went to picking hops again.

I was there about two months. When the picking was finished, I left for Sacramento and hung around there for a week before I made up my mind to go back to 'Frisco. I took the same boat ride as when I came from town. I rode until I was near Stockton, changed my mind, and got off. It's quite a way from the river to Stockton, and I was walking.

When I came to a farm, I saw a man working in a beet field, and I asked for work. He asked me if I had ever done that kind of work. I said, "Yes," for I had worked in the beet fields of Colorado. The man hired me right away. There were Mexicans, Filipinos, and three Indian boys working there. The Indians were Zunis and not used to hard work. The Zunis are all small men. When I was in school in Santa Fe, they wanted to do the easy jobs.

101

The beets were dug out by machine, and the men cut the tops off with a bolo knife. The beets were big and heavy, and it was hard work, for you bent down all day and you had to be fast. I wasn't very fast, but I tried to keep up with the other boys. The boss was a Spaniard—mean, too. Our food was not very good, and most of the days were cloudy, rainy, and uncomfortable. Although it rained hard, we had to keep working. I did not like working there so I decided to quit. There were plenty of jobs at that time—I guess because they didn't pay much.

I was friendly with the Zuni boys, and I told them I was going to Stockton to look for another job. They all wanted to quit. I said, "You don't have to quit just because I quit"; but they did. The last day was rainy. We stayed in camp waiting to get our pay. There was a little Mexican boy smoking something behind the bunkhouse. When I rounded the corner, he tried to hide something behind him. I asked him in Spanish what he was hiding. He showed me a cigarette; then he pointed to a tree which was nine feet tall. There were four of these behind the house. They had been there a long time, and the plants looked like regular trees. I asked him what they were, and he said, "Marijuana."

I told the Indian boys, and one of them wanted to try it. The Mexican boy gave him a cigarette. He puffed it a few times, but felt nothing. Then he inhaled some more, and he began to laugh his head off. We tried to stop him, but he laughed even more. The other boys wanted to pick some of the leaves, so we all filled our pockets to take them along. That was the first time I had seen marijuana—I had just heard about it before. I never smoked nor drank strong stuff.

After we got our pay, we walked away from camp in the rain. We walked about a mile to catch the bus. This boy kept laughing all the way and on the bus to Stockton. Everybody thought he must be crazy. When we got to town, we found a room and locked him in—still laughing. Two days later, I decided to throw the leaves in a trash can. When I told a Mexican, he looked, but the trash can had been emptied.

I hung around for a week and made up my mind to go to Fresno. The Indian boys stayed in Stockton. I stopped in a town called Riverbank, close to Modesto. There was roundhouse for the Santa Fe trains. I asked for a job, and I was hired to work nights. I helped the boiler washer and later the boiler maker. I liked those jobs, and I got along just fine. I was surprised to find three more Zuni boys working there. They all lived in box cars, and I moved into one. While I was in Riverbank, I joined the Disabled American Veterans.

I was there a few months when a machinist boss saw us Indian boys throwing a baseball around, and he wanted to organize a team. He asked if we were good players. Some could play, but most of the team which we formed were white boys. I was the catcher, and a man from Oakdale, an old-timer, pitched. He used to play in the Coast League. Anyway, we got suits and played teams around the area.

The shop needed more Indian workers, so I sent to Litchfield, Arizona, for my brother, Grover. I sent the fare money and he arrived in a few days. After working a year at Riverbank, I decided to visit my folks at

Litchfield. It was the summer of 1924, and I had not seen my mother since I left for China in 1919, and my father was dead now. I thought that I would soon be back to Riverbank, but, once in Arizona, I stayed with my family.

For the trip home I sent my suitcase on ahead to Phoenix, for I planned to catch a ride on the trains. While in Riverbank, I met a Pima boy from the Sacaton Indian Reservation. His name was Nelson—a little, short man. I told him I was going to Arizona, and right away he wanted to go, but he had no money. I knew how to steal rides on trains, and I told him that we would grab a ride on a passenger train. He did not like the idea. I told him, "You don't have to come if you don't want to." Finally he made up his mind, for he wanted to go home bad.

That night we watched the trains and saw where to hide so we could jump on just as the train started. I showed him where to sit on the steps so as not to be seen. A passenger train stopped, and we jumped on just as it started. The train stopped at Indio, and we got off before it reached the station. When it started, we jumped on once more. I saw two policemen watching for riders, but they did not see us. We travelled on to Yuma, and there we almost got caught. The railroad bulls saw us and chased us into the brush, but they lost us because it was night. We were sure scared. The Pima boy was so scared that for awhile he did not want to ride again. We waited for two nights, and he decided to go. The next ride took us to Phoenix. I don't remember how I got from there to the Pima reservation.

At Sacaton I decided to go visit my cousin, Mrs. José Queen. When I was about a hundred yards from her home, I met my brother Nicolás and his family. They were going to a little place called Liberty, near Buckeye. They asked me to go with them to pick cotton there. I thought that I might just as well go with them. I had not seen my brother since he left the Santa Fe school in 1913. He was now married and had three daughters. They had a light wagon which was all loaded and pulled by a horse. They also had a donkey with them. It belonged to an old chief, José Foot, who was now in jail, so my brother was caring for the donkey for him.

At that time (1924) there were not many good roads. We drove toward Phoenix, and we stopped that night at the Guadalupe Yaqui Indian Village. Later this area would be the corner of Base Line Road and I-10, but then was just orange groves. Next morning we passed through Phoenix and got on the Buckeye Road. There were very few cars on the roads, so, while the going was slow, we made it to Liberty and found the cotton pickers' camp. There were some of our Indian people already there. I picked cotton with them for awhile; then I joined my family at Litchfield Park.

My family worked for the Goodyear Company Farms. My oldest brother, José, had joined the company in 1916 and had become the boss of the cotton pickers. Two other brothers worked as mule skinners, cultivating cotton. My mother, sister, and brother John, called Shorty, worked picking cotton. The Goodyear Company kept moving the family around to different farms. At first they worked in Goodyear, Arizona, a one-store, company village. They had a long line of adobe buildings, called Camp 1, where the workers lived. Most of the workers were Papagos, but there were some Mexican families as well. Later my folks were moved to Camp 2, just east of Goodyear. Still later the whole camp moved to another farm called Litchfield Park, about twenty-two miles west of Phoenix. The workers and families were carried in wagons pulled by mules. The extra mules were walked over. They didn't have big trucks to haul people and mules like they have now. I was not at home during these times, but the family told me about them.

The farms were run by two brothers. Mr. Elias Morris was the company boss. He was a big man, probably 6′6″ and 295 pounds. He was a nice man. His brother, Harvey, was married to a Mexican woman. When I came to visit my family, I just made myself at home and did not do anything. Mr. Elias Morris asked my brother if I had just gotten out of the Army. Then one day he asked me if I wanted to work. When I said, "Yes," he gave me a job as a cotton weightman. That was the easiest job I ever had. First thing in the morning I would hitch up two mules and pull the loaded cotton to the gin. I liked the job, but it was hot. Well, in my young days, I did not mind the heat because my skin was already cooked like a steak. When I got older, I couldn't stand the heat, so I had a cooler like the white people.

As farm workers, we were paid $1.50 a day and board. All the money we made we put into one bank—my mother. Any time one of us needed some money, we went to her. We always had plenty, and we always had eats, even when other people were short of things. Sometimes Papagos and Mexicans would come to Mama and ask for something. It was hard, though, after the cotton picking was all over. There was not much other work around there until spring-time, when the fields had to be plowed again.

After the cotton harvest was about over, I decided to make a trip to the Big Reservation to visit my relatives there. Most of the villages north of Sells seemed like one big family, and all of the villagers were relatives. I had not been on the reservation since my cousin, Car-me, took me to Littlefield and Cababi villages in 1902 when I was only seven.

I told Mother that I wanted to go and that I wished to stay there for awhile. Ma consented. I loaded my bedding and a few clothes in a Model-T Ford that we had. The car had no top. I left Litchfield and headed for Phoenix. At that time there were few cars (but lots of wagons) in Phoenix, so it was safer to go through. I stopped for awhile and bought something to eat. Everything was cheap in those days. Then I drove to Casa Grande, which was a small town. There was a main street facing the railroad depot. On the other side of the tracks was a grocery, a little store run by a Chinaman. I bought a few things to take along, filled up the gas tank, and started off on a dusty road into the reservation.

At that time there were only wagon roads on the reservation, and they were all dusty and crooked. The Chuichu Village road was very bad all the way. I came to a little village called Klamaka. I did not stop long, but drove on to Anegam and then to Santa Rosa, the largest village in the area (about forty miles from Casa Grande). Santa Rosa was about three miles from Littlefield, my birthplace. Santa Rosa was a growing Indian community in the early 1970s, while Littlefield had only two families. By the mid-1980s Littlefield was completely gone. The old people had died off and their grown children had moved — many to Tucson.

I passed through Santa Rosa to a village called Circle Walk by the Papagos. It was my mother's birthplace, and all the people there were my relatives. Since my visit in 1902, the village had moved north half a mile, but only a few people lived there; some had made their new home at Covered Wells — seven or eight miles away. Soon I drove on to San Louis and stopped to drink some water. I knew some of those people, and all of them knew my mother. Then I drove to another village, San Luis, where our senior chief lived; it was also the place of my mother and father's old ranch before they moved to Tucson. In 1915, my parents still had many cattle there. My younger brother, Nicolás, had taken it over. Later he married and went to his father-in-law's place high up on the mountains.

When Nicolás left, my father's brother began to look after the cattle while my parents were living at Goodyear and Litchfield Park. He would never tell them how he was doing out there. My uncle used to come to Litchfield Park to get his supplies. The family bought him fifty-pound sacks of flour, one-hundred-pound sacks of green coffee, and one hundred pounds of sugar. He had their horses, and they bought him new harness and a wagon, and gave him money for things needed at the ranch. Sometime later they heard from friends visiting the reservation that he had gambled away their money. He was selling the supplies and cattle at Ajo and losing everything. By that time, almost all of the cattle were gone. Afterward my uncle died suddenly, but we didn't learn how it happened.

In 1970, when I visited the area with my wife, the few houses at the ranch looked empty. From one house a man came out, which surprised us. He was Val-Leea, my uncle's son. I asked him if any more people lived there. He said, "No, I'm the only one who lives here." We talked to him about the place. I told him that my folks used to live there, and I pointed to their old adobe house. Val-Leea was looking after the few cattle that had belonged to his brother, Steven, and his sister. The Papagos had nicknamed Steven "Part Yellow." Steven's sister always seemed to have plenty of money and spent it having a good time in Tucson. When Steven came back from California, he found that she was selling their cattle and using the money for drinking. He chased her away, and she died in Tucson from drinking too much wine. Later Steven was also found dead from drinking wine.

My drive from Litchfield Park ended at Big Field Village, where I stayed with my uncle, nicknamed Sweet Mouth. After some days of visiting, he took me to see how they made rain. The medicine men started at Nolia Village and tried to find out when the rain would come. People from different villages gathered there to help out. The men put up four corner posts, strung rope in between, and hung small eagle feathers all around. The medicine men sat in the middle and sang while the people danced around them in a circle. My uncle and I took part in the dancing.

Once during every dance a medicine man would examine the feathers for moisture, and sometimes, when he shook the string, it would sprinkle. He would then say, "The rain will come from the north (or east)." After awhile, a man would bring a big bucketful of cactus wine. Each person would get a cupful to drink. It was not strong, and people did not get drunk. I tasted it, but I didn't drink. They kept up the dancing, checking, and drinking all night long. In the morning, after the rain dance was over, we went back home like the rest of the people.

While I was with my uncle Sweet Mouth, he wanted me to go to a meeting at Chief José Foot's place. I had never been to a Papago meeting, and I was interested. The old chief had gone to the Santa Fe Indian School, but he had not learned much. He couldn't read or speak English very well. I guess that they brought me to the meeting because they thought that I knew more English and could read and translate a letter the chief had received from Phoenix. My education was only to the eighth grade, but I had been around some and had picked up more English. I read the note and tried to explain to the chief what it said as best I could. At the meeting there was a bad medicine man, who was feared by all the people. He did not believe that I had explained the letter to them. (This man ran off all the people who lived in his village. He has been dead for many years now. His ranch was taken over by his son, who was later run over by a car and killed at Sahuarita.)

Sometime later my uncle wanted to move up to visit my family's home ranch. There were three families there, including my brother Nicolás and his family, who had returned from picking cotton. Nick and I would climb the mountains when we had nothing else to do. Sometimes his whole family would load in a wagon and go shopping in Sells. By this time the wine-drinking festival had begun. People began at one village and moved on from village to village. The wine drinking was now going on at Iron Stand, and Uncle Sweet Mouth told the whole family to get ready to travel to that village to drink wine. I did not have much to carry, but I helped pack their things. Iron Stand was the village where many years before the Apaches had massacred the old and young, as my mother used to tell.

We arrived at Iron Stand and put up a little tent. People went from house to house for drinks. Already there were many drunks all over. I could not sleep at night, for all of the drunks were hollering and singing. Soon I was getting hungry. Because everybody was drinking, no one was cooking. Next morning I decided to leave without letting them know. Besides, I didn't see any of the family anywhere. I thought that I would go to San Luis Village, where I knew some people.

I left carrying my .38-caliber rifle, and walked through the desert toward a mountain where I knew San Luis was located. The distance was about ten miles. I arrived there in the afternoon. Right away a ten-year-old boy named Fernando saw me coming. He met me and asked, "Where did you come from?" I said, "Iron Stand Village." He took me to his home. His mother was there, and she was surprised to see me. I had not seen her for a long time. She used to live in Tucson when she was a young girl before her marriage. She was one of the fastest runners in track. She also asked me where I came from. I told her that I came from Iron Stand. "You know, where the wine drinking is going on." She knew. She asked me why I left, and I told her that I never drank. Besides, I could not sleep, and I had nothing to eat because everybody was drunk, so I had decided to leave and go to Tucson. She asked me to stay till the next day. I thanked her, but I was anxious to keep going. I left my rifle with them. "Use it to hunt," I said. "Someday I will come back and get the gun." Some years later, I did.

That evening I decided to walk to Big Field Village, another ten miles. Fernando went along for a distance, then turned back. (When Fernando grew up and got married, he worked at the Ajo mine, but he died when he was twenty-eight years old. By the early 1970s his wife was gone and only his father, an old man, was living in Big Field Village.) That night I slept under a tree and next morning I tried to crank my Model-T. I was afraid it wouldn't start, but I kept cranking it. Finally it started. I was glad.

I drove to Sells, a village which used to be called Indian Oasis. I bought some gasoline and headed for Tucson. The Ford was going twenty miles an hour, and in those days we thought that a car going that speed was too fast. I don't remember how long it took me to get to Tucson because I had no watch.

At that time, our people were scattered all over south Tucson. I went to see my cousin, Car-me, and her daughter, Rose Lucas. They were glad to see me. I told them I would stay one night there and leave in the morning for Litchfield Park. Next morning, both of them went to their work. I drove through Florence to Blackwater, in the Gila River Pima Reservation, and then to Sacaton, where I rested. I got to thinking about my cousin from Santa Rosa who lived on the other side of the Gila River in the Santana District. She was the daughter of an old chief, Con-nee-Law, and her husband was a Pima named José Queen. They had two children and one of their boys was married to a Pima girl. The chief was the organizer of ceremonies and, after he died around 1930, it seemed that everything changed. There were no more Indian festivals, games, or dances.

One time Con-nee-Law came to visit his daughter with his old wife. She was over ninety, and he was even older. There were four great grandchildren there, for a total of fifteen people in one big room in an old, adobe house. I was one of them. Everybody slept on the dirt floor except José Queen and his wife, who slept on an old, spring bed. That night the old chief was lying near the doorway when his wife felt something touch her feet. She jumped up quick. One girl was yelling that something was crawling on her feet. Everybody got up quickly. One girl was standing on the table hollering, "Grandpa!" Grandpa paid no attention. He was lying still, without a shirt on. It was very warm inside, and a rattlesnake went over his body. He never moved. I got a stick and hit it, and José helped to kill the snake. After that, we all laughed our heads off at the old chief. We also laughed at the girl on the table and how she got there so quickly. Then the grandchildren asked the old man how it felt with a snake crawling on his body. He said, "I felt something crawling. I did not know it was a snake, but I just lay there." Everybody laughed again.

José Queen was a great music man. He played a violin whenever there was a dance. They had another uncle living with them, called Sharp Hat, who was about seventy-eight years old. He was still very lively and a good *pascola* dancer. People used to hire him to dance at their fiestas.

While I was at Queen's place, Sharp Hat told us that he was trying to get San José, one of only seven story-tellers left, to come tell the story about the old people who lived at Casa Grande ruins long ago. San José came and told Sharp Hat to sharpen a long stick in case some of the seven listeners fell asleep while he told of the fighting of the Casa Grande people against another tribe. If someone went to sleep, he would jab him with the stick. He said, "That's the way the old storytellers did it." Sometimes a storyteller would paint a man's face if he went to sleep.

The story went on all night until morning, and then it was begun again that night. The storytellers only tell their stories at night. It was a long story, and I was so tired that I could hardly keep my eyes open. I wanted to learn the story, but I was so sleepy that I didn't learn much. Neither did the others. Still, it was an interesting story.

José Queen had a big patch of watermelons, chilis, pumpkins, beans, and corn. One day he told me about the time when someone was stealing his melons and corn. "They were about all gone. I guess they stole them during the night while I was sleeping soundly." In the mornings, he would go and look at the patch and see broken stalks and rinds all over the field. One night he did not go to sleep; instead, he hid in the middle of the field and waited quite awhile. About midnight the thieves came, all spread out. When they got closer, he got up and stood around like he was one of them. Soon, one of the boys came over to him and said in a low voice, "Hey, the melons are about all gone. I can't find one." Queen said, "Ya, because you guys steal them all." The boy was surprised when he recognized the owner. He tried to tell him that this was his first time there. Queen said, "I think you are the leader of this gang of thieves." They left fast and never came back again. We laughed as he told about it.

I enjoyed my visit with José Queen; then I returned to my family at Litchfield Park. There was little work to be found, so my brother John, my sister, Sarah, my mother, and I went to Ajo, Arizona. John and I were hired right away to work in the Phelps-Dodge pit mine. We rented a house in Clarktown and moved in.

Most of the men in the pit mine were Papagos. Everything was done by hand. They drilled, shoveled, and moved track. It was hard work at first, but John and I got used to it. A few months later I was hurt while carrying a big water pump with three other boys. One stumbled on a rock and fell. The weight shifted and pulled my shoulder muscle, so I was taken to the hospital for treatment. I stayed for awhile, but my younger brother continued working.

I was hurt three more times at the mine. I smashed my hand when a rail dropped on it. I was knocked down by a dump truck, along with a number of other boys. Most of us were hurt. I almost broke my back, and my body was all swollen and blue. My mother was at her place in Coolidge, and I went there and stayed. She treated me. A doctor from the Pima reservation could not do anything for me but give me some pills, and they did no good. However, in a few weeks I was all right, and I went back to Ajo and started to work again.

The last injury was while I was pushing an iron mine-cart loaded with rocks on a high hill above the mill. The track was supposed to be blocked, but it was night and the switchman had gone to sleep. The cart picked up speed and was going down toward the dumping point where there was a three-hundred-foot drop-off. Another boy was on the cart with me, and he yelled for me to jump but I couldn't — my pants and belt were caught, and I couldn't get loose. Just when the cart was about to jump off the cliff, he caught me around the neck and pulled me backward off the cart. We fell fifteen feet onto the rocks. The cart plunged down to three hundred feet below.

I don't know how long we lay there on the rocks. I remember my friend pulled me up. Our boss heard the noise and was looking for us just when we came up. We were all bloody, and our clothes were torn. The boss asked what happened; I told him, and he sent us home. It was midnight.

In the morning my mother saw my clothes were bloody and all torn up. She was shocked. I was bruised all over my body and very sore. I did not want to go to the doctor, but Mama forced me to, and the doctor told me to lay off a few weeks. The company did not give me any pay while I was resting. My mother did not want me to work at the mine again. So after two weeks I decided to quit. I went to see my boss and told him that I intended to go to California and find work there that was not so dangerous.

The boss was a good man. He had been a captain in the Army overseas, and he said he would give me a letter to show wherever I went. I told him that I was going to Fresno, where I had been before. I knew a man in the employment office there. I still have that letter which was given to me in Ajo on July 3, 1924, by Captain William J. H. Hubbard, 1st U.S. Division, A.E.F.

We told the owner of our rented house that we were going to California. We said that we would leave our things in the house and that we would pay our rent every month. We had a new car so we had no trouble driving to California. We went by way of Yuma to Los Angeles, then along the coastal highway. My mother had never seen the ocean before. It was July and there was so much fog that sometimes we could hardly see the highway. We turned off on the road to Fresno, and it was warm in the San Joaquin Valley.

In Fresno we went right away to the employment office to see the big man. I knew him. I told him that I had brought my whole family from Ajo. He called somebody and then asked if we wanted to work tomorrow; we said, "Yes." Next morning we reported to a farmer to turn the cantaloupe vines from the furrows.

In August the employment man sent us to Hollister, near the coast, to pick prunes. The place was cold nights. We worked for a month until the crop was about finished. The employment man called us back to Fresno in September to pick grapes, so we went to a place across the San Joaquin River, a few miles from town. There were some Indians there, and we camped with them along the river. My folks had never picked grapes before, and they liked the job very much. They also ate plenty of them. We picked there for two months; then, at the end of October, we left for Arizona and Magdalena, Sonora, Mexico. Our boss asked us to come back next year.

It was about the time when our people worship in Mexico, so my folks wanted to go. Our trip back was good all the way. We stopped in Ajo to check our house. Everything seemed to be all right, so we left for Nogales and Magdalena. There were already thousands of people there, and still more were coming to worship. Afterward we decided to visit Hermosillo. I saw some Papagos who lived there in Mexico. I took many snapshots of my family.

I guess that we spent two weeks in Mexico, and then we came back to Ajo. I did not want to work in the mine. My family wanted to go back to Litchfield Park, where my oldest brother worked. We loaded our things from the house in Ajo, and drove away. I did not want to go back to Litchfield Park, so I stopped off in Tucson.

A man who was hiring mule skinners there wanted twenty Papagos for highway work near the San Carlos Dam, and I was hired. That night the workers, some with families, loaded on a truck. Our boss had a wooden leg, and some of the boys asked, "Can he drive with a wooden leg?" Everybody laughed. He could, but it was slow going all night, and rough. We got in the next morning and camped in tents across a little river from San Carlos Village. Some of us had no blankets, so we gathered some dry grass and paper for bedding.

After we were all settled down, the boss showed us the mules. Each man picked out four mules for his plow or fresno, which was an earth-moving scoop. Most of those boys had not gone to school; I was the only one who understood English, so I spoke to the boss for them. I worked for over four months and got along just fine until a new foreman came to boss us. He was mean. If a boy slowed down a little, he'd holler. He always carried a blacksnake whip, and one day he used it on a boy. It made all the boys mad. Next day he hit a boy with a chain. That noon I spoke to the Big Boss, a lady, about what happened. I told her that the man whipped the boys like mules and that we wouldn't take that kind of treatment. We quit. The lady asked us to stay until Saturday, and we did. Then we got our pay and left.

That night I caught a freight train to Miami, Arizona, a mining town. I spent two days there, then took a bus to Phoenix. There I was hired again to do road building near Florence. I had four mules and a fresno; there were no tractors to bank the dirt like today. There were about thirty Papago boys on that job. Our foreman at Florence had another job at Wellton, Arizona. I went along, and my friend Nestro Francisco and my brother Grover came to join us. They loaded the mules and workers in boxcars for the trip. The job in Wellton was leveling fields and pulling mesquite stumps. It's a hard job to pull stumps, and I had eight mules. Later that cleared area became part of some large farms. I worked there for two months and then quit because the boss could not pay us. They said he went broke. Many Papagos with families worked there, and I was sorry for them. I was by myself so it was not so hard.

I had saved a little cash, and I decided to buy a used Model-T Ford in Phoenix. I paid the full price for it, seventy-five dollars, and headed for California again. When we drove through El Centro, the cylinder head cracked. I was lucky that it happened near a section house where a Mexican family lived. At first I didn't know what to do. The section man came over to see what happened, and I showed him the cracked head. He helped me to find a new head, and I got a man to help me put it on. The Mexican family were nice people and I slept and ate with them for five days. I tried to pay them, but they didn't want any money for the eats. They told me that I needed the money more than they did. I thanked everybody.

I drove on and the next day I arrived in Los Angeles. It was Sunday, and I knew where the Indians hung out. Right away I found a friend. He told me that he lived in Burbank and worked with mule teams. I went with him and got a job grading land. I got a plow that used six mules and took two men to hold it down. Burbank wasn't much of a town then—one drugstore and one grocery. When I took my family in 1949 to see the place where I worked in 1925, I couldn't recognize it.

I worked there for four months, and I boarded with a Mexican family. When our work was almost finished, they began to lay us off. The employment office in town had plenty of jobs for laborers at that time. Labor was cheap, but so were many things in the stores. I used to eat in small places. A bowl of beans and a cup of coffee would cost from fifteen to thirty-five cents. Rooms were fifty cents a night. After I was laid off, I didn't look for another job. I just took it easy for awhile and went around town spending money with my friends.

Sometimes a man came asking Indian boys to take parts in movies, playing the part of Indians. I took a part one time in winter. We had almost no clothes on, and they wouldn't let us start a fire. I almost froze. I only hired for the movies one time—no more. They paid us four dollars a day, but I wanted a different kind of job. I didn't play Indian again.

One Sunday, an Indian man asked a Papago friend and me if we wanted work. I asked, "What kind of work?" He said, "Work in a salmon cannery in Alaska." I told him that I didn't want to go up there because it was too cold. My friend also turned him down. Later, I began to think about it, and after two days I decided that I might just as well go to Alaska and see it—snow, Eskimos, and all. I always liked to go places—that's why I volunteered for France, China, and the Philippine Islands. Next time I saw the man, I told him that I wanted to sign up. My friend was not around, so I could not tell him that I was going to Alaska.

Two days passed, and then the man told me that we

121

would leave that night. A big truck, loaded with men, picked me up. We rode all night, and in the early morning we were along the San Francisco waterfront. I saw a small, three-masted boat. Some of the men who had been to Alaska before said, "That's the boat we are going in."

The men were told they could buy heavy clothing, shoes, blankets, and other things on credit, so many men bought things. A man told me not to buy on credit because they took all your money—either charged you too much or cheated you—so I did not buy anything. I had my suitcase with me, and I had plenty of clothes. I was glad later that I took the man's word. I guess that all the clothes and things belonged to some Chinese, because they also sold cocaine, opium, and marijuana on the boat. There were all kinds of people on that boat—Mexicans, Negroes, Chinese, Filipinos, Italians, and Anglos. We loaded next day, the sailors pulled up the sails, and we headed for the Golden Gate. Everybody stood on deck to say goodbye to San Francisco.

A few days out, I woke up and went up on deck. I thought that the windjammer was moving but, to my surprise, the boat was standing still. The ocean was just as smooth as glass. The boat drifted for two days. Then, as we slept, the boat began moving—too much. A storm had come up and it rocked the boat up and down; it rolled and rolled. The captain told us all to stay in bed and tie ourselves down with our belts. Many of the men were seasick, and some were pretty scared. I did not mind the motion so much because I had crossed the Atlantic Ocean twice, the Pacific twice, and the Yellow Sea several times. That old sergeant in the Army had told me how not to get seasick, so I got along all right.

The windjammer was small and mostly we stayed in the hold, so it was a tiresome ride the way we were packed in there. There was fighting going on between the men all the time. Some days were stormy, others calm. It took us about a month to get to Alaska. One morning when I woke up, the ship was still; it felt like it was not moving. I went up on deck just in time to see a small boat chasing a whale. A big harpoon gun on the front of the boat was used to shoot the whale. When the ship came close to us, I could see a dead whale tied up on each side of it. There was a little house on its deck where they pulled the whale up and cut off the fat with long knives. Then there was a stove to melt the fat. I had never seen anything like that before.

After a month on the ship, I saw a mountain with smoke on top and fire coming out. A man said, "That's Alaska." Our sailboat was standing still, just drifting for two and a half days. Then I saw three more sailboats, about our size, ahead of us. The boats had to go through a narrow channel and it was hard to do when there was no wind. I watched one boat try to go through the channel; then, suddenly, it circled back to the place where it started. Those boats kept trying, but until the wind came up they didn't make it. On the third day the boats went straight through the opening. That afternoon it was our turn. We tried, but the boat turned short, made a circle, and tried again. The second time we went through. The place where we were going was not very far away, but the boat sailed very slowly. In the distance it looked like the mouth of a large river with houses on each side.

We reached shore at 7 P.M., but it was still as light as in the afternoon. I was surprised because it never got dark. The boat tied up at a pier, and I was glad to get off. A man showed us where to stay. We lived in a two-story building. I was the only Indian boy in the crowd. Some of the men had been there before, and they knew the works. Next morning they told the men what each would do. They gave me the the job of loading salmon cans in a little pushcart. Some men worked at machines packing the salmon in cans. A little way from the cannery were many fishing boats. I guess there were more than fifty of them. They brought salmon in twice a day. I had never seen salmon before.

I guess that there were about fifty workers and almost all of them used marijuana or cocaine. The Chinamen had opium. Once in a while, a man would become wild because of his use of marijuana. Once, two Mexicans fought with knives. They cut each other very badly, and one died in a short time. I guess somebody called the police, for the F.B.I. came and found the Mexican who had killed the other man. He was hiding behind a fisherman's building. They took him across the river to police headquarters.

The next week some men came who looked like mountain men, with long beards. They didn't look like police, but we found out that they were F.B.I. men. They went to the building where we lived and started searching. They started at the top floor, then went down to where all of the Chinese were quartered. I guess the Chinamen knew they were going to be searched. They ran out in all directions and carried some things which they threw into the tall weeds. The agents took some Chinese away. Later, I walked out to see what was there, and I found a jar which looked like a small Indian olla. I opened it. In it was some black stuff which looked like roof tar. I told a friend, a Mexican boy from Tucson, what I found. I did not know that it was opium, for I had never seen it before. He wanted to take it but was afraid to. Other boys looked around in the tall grass. Some found pistols, knives, Chinese pipes, more opium, and some white powder. That was some excitement that day.

One day, one of the firemen was very sick and had to be taken somewhere to be treated. Our boss came around and asked the men if anyone knew how to fire boilers. Nobody seemed to know the fireman's job. When he asked me, I told him I didn't know, but later I told a friend that I used to work the boilers in school, although it was a long time ago. The boss must have heard, for he came back to me. I told him I was not sure because it was so long ago, but I said, "I'll try." He watched me to see if I remembered what to do. I filled the boilers with water, checked the meters, and fired the boilers. The boss watched and said I was hired. I worked alone. I loaded coal in a wheelbarrow and dumped it in front of the fireboxes. There were eight boilers to look after. It was hot there, and I usually worked with my shirt off.

The boss, a German, was a good man. He came again at midnight to relieve me. I was glad afterward that I got that job because they paid me more than working in the cannery. They also brought me meals each shift—and plenty, too. I could not eat it all, and it was better than what the boys ate. When I was relieved at midnight, I was surprised that it was still daylight, so I just walked on the beach. I did not feel sleepy, for it never got dark. I saw many men just doing things like in the daytime.

Sometimes I walked along the big river. The first time I walked about a mile north, and I saw an Eskimo village with women and huskies, which barked at me. As soon as the women saw me, they all ran inside. I don't know what they called their homes, but they looked like a badger's hole. Their men worked in the canneries or at fishing, but the women stayed at home like prairie dogs. I watched the Eskimos hanging salmon to dry.

There were plenty of mosquitos, big as house flies. The company gave each man a net to wear over his hat and face. It was supposed to protect him from mosquito bites. They also told us not to walk on the grass because of quicksand in some places; at our place they had boardwalks to all the buildings. One night as I was walking along the beach, I saw a little tree. I thought, "I'll cut a branch and make something with my knife, a cane." I knelt down and cut it. When I came back to camp, somebody asked me what happened, for there was blood all over my face. When I took my heavy clothing off, I saw blood on my body also. It was from mosquito bites, but they did not itch.

I spent most of the time by myself, for I did not trust the other men—everyone smoked marijuana. After work, some of the men, especially the Mexicans, would play music and dance by themselves, for there were no women. One day one of the boys said that we ought to do something to have some fun — play ball or something. He made a rag ball to play with, but I had a real ball and a glove in my suitcase. Along the river were a lot of Filipinos, and how they loved to play ball! We formed a team, and soon we had a game with a cannery two miles away. We all walked two miles to that place, and we had a good time.

One time after work I was walking along the beach when I saw two men walking in my direction. Each of them had long hair that seemed to have grown three or four months; they looked like hippies, but they had no beards. I passed them close, but I did not recognize either. One of them limped. I thought, "They must be Eskimos," but I tried to think where I had seen a man limp like that before. I walked as far as another cannery and then headed back home. I saw these two men coming my way, and I decided to speak to them. They kept looking at me. I first spoke in Spanish, and when we recognized each other, we laughed our hearts out. "We never expected to see you in Alaska." One was a Papago boy I had worked with, and he had been with me when I first said that I wouldn't go to Alaska. The other, named Manuel, was also a Papago. One was from Tucson, the other from the Big Reservation. I told my friends that I had thought that I was the only Papago in Alaska. We were very happy to be together again.

I joked with them and told them that I had thought they were Eskimos because of their long hair. They laughed at that. They said, "Nobody has scissors to cut our hair, so we look dangerous." Right away they asked me if I had scissors. "Ya, I got scissors to cut my own hair." We walked back to my place, and I cut their hair close. They said, "Boy, it sure feels good to have short hair again. If it wasn't for you, our hair would grow as long as a woman's hair." And we laughed some more.

They asked me what I did at the cannery, and I told them that I worked as a fireman. My shift was until midnight, when I was brought a big basket of food. I told my friends that I worked alone and invited them to come help me eat that big basket of food. They came next evening about 10 P.M., and they came often thereafter.

I stayed in Alaska about five or six months. It was getting darker; I think it was September when they told us to get ready to go back to the States. Before we left, my boss asked me to come back as fireman next year. When we were told to load, I was glad. We got on the same windjammer, and once more the trip took about a month. Sometimes the ocean was as smooth as glass; other times it would rain and blow and the waves would cover the boat.

At the San Francisco pier, everybody got his pay. I was sorry for some of the boys who got very little pay because of credit. Some got almost nothing. I was happy that I had bought nothing from them and I had gotten the job as fireman, which paid more than in the cannery. My two Papago friends did not get much pay. After payday we separated, and I hung around for a week at the Y.M.C.A. There were plenty of jobs written all over the board at the employment office. A laborer's job paid $1.50 a day. Men were wanted in South America by the Armour Packing Company. It made me think; I had always wanted to see South America. I decided to stay in town, but I wanted something different from skinning mules.

One day I rode a streetcar to south San Francisco and asked for a job at the Armour Packing House. I was hired, and the boss sent me to the basement, where they piled the cowhides. A dozen men worked there. It was heavy work putting those hides in piles five feet high. I worked there for about a month; then they took me out of the basement and gave me a job in the "hot dog" factory. There they made all kinds of meat—bologna, hot dogs, sausage, and canned meats. They gave me a cart on which to load the bologna and hot dogs. There were hundreds of men and women working in that plant.

I moved from the Y.M.C.A. to a hotel, but I always spent my evenings at the Y.M.C.A.—I never went to town. After work, one evening while I was reading a newspaper, a Navajo boy named Engeno came to talk to me. He asked where I worked, and I told him. I also asked him where he worked, and he didn't know what to say. He never worked. I had known people like him at school—afraid of work. He just hung around. I don't know how he ate. Every time I came to the "Y," he'd be there, and he'd never leave me. One evening I came back from work and he was in my room. I was surprised that he got in. Maybe he lied to the landlord to get a key. He was dirty and lying on my bed; I did not like it, but I said nothing.

I had a good job, and the Armour Company put a notice on a board wanting men in Argentina. Right away, I signed up to go there, but I changed my mind in the last few days before we were supposed to leave. Instead, I decided to go to Portland, Oregon. The Navajo man found out that I had quit my job, and he asked me where I was going. I did not want to tell him, but I felt kind of sorry for him. I told him, and he said that he knew Portland very well. "I've been there and also to the Toppenish Indian Reservation in Washington." So I paid our fare to Portland by bus.

When we arrived we hung around, but I did not look for a job. The Navajo told me that he wanted to go to Toppenish and that he knew somebody there. He was sure we could get a job there or that the Indian agent would help us find a job, so we left Portland, hiking. I carried my suitcase. Just outside of town, a man gave us a lift. He was a salesman heading for Walla Walla. He was a good man, and I was glad for that ride. I was carrying the cane that I had carved in Alaska of some kind of wood. When he let us out, I wanted him to take the cane. He liked it and asked me where I got it. I told him that I made it in Alaska. He said that it was too nice to accept, but finally he took it and was pleased.

It was winter and very cold in Toppenish when we got there. We did not know where to sleep, so we went to see the Indian agent. Engeno knew where the office was, but when we got there he was afraid to talk. The agent asked me what tribe I belonged to, and I told him, "Papago." He knew the Papagos very well for he used to be an agent on the Navajo Reservation. I told him that I was sorry I had left my good job in San Francisco, but that I wanted to see Washington State. He told me that the town of Toppenish was very small and there was not much work around. They have a short summer and in other seasons there wasn't much to do. The agent found us a place to stay. That night, it snowed.

Next day the agent called an Indian policeman named John and asked him to keep us at his place until he could find what to do with us. He promised John groceries to help, so John took us in his Model-T to his home. John was a very fine man, about 6′3″. He asked me many things—where I came from, what I did. John had a wife and three children. They were a nice family, kind. John told us we could stay. Every day I went with John around the reservation. Sometimes we would go to the sick. Many people would be there and dance and sing around the sick person. But this Navajo would never go with us.

When we were well acquainted, John told me about a big Indian powwow at Spokane. He asked me to go with him to see the many tribes who came there. We left Toppenish in the morning and travelled all day. His Model-T had no top so it was a cold ride. I had no overcoat, so the policeman lent me a blanket to wrap around me. We arrived in the evening. First we found a room and then we went around. I walked around town in the blanket. I did not feel right because at home my people never do that because it is warm.

Next day there was a big parade. Then we went to where the Indians had cleared the ground and had a big tent like the circus. Inside there was entertainment of all kinds. At the powwow Haskell Indian School of Kansas was playing a football game against Gonzaga University of Washington. All Indians got in free. Haskell beat Gonzaga. I was surprised to see a boy I used to know in Phoenix Indian School on the Haskell team. His name was Jack Norton, and he was surprised to see me. "Long way from home," he said. "What are you doing up here? Why don't you come to Haskell and play football?" I told him I was too old to go to school. He laughed at my saying I was an old man.

I did not have a good time in Spokane, for I was too cold and often stayed indoors. After three days we decided to go home. It was December when we left Spokane, and there was a lot of snow on the ground. More eagles were sitting on the fence posts than I had ever seen before. I was glad to get back to Toppenish. While we had been gone, the Navajo boy had done nothing but sleep. One day Mrs. John asked him to cut some wood. He did not want to cut wood, and he said he didn't know how. John's wife got mad and ran him off. When we came back, John asked his wife about Engeno. She told him what happened, and I told him what kind of a man he was.

By this time, many Indian people in the Toppenish Reservation knew me, even though I was not one of them. They were very nice people. Everywhere I went with Policeman John, I was welcomed. One day, John asked me if I knew how to handle horses and a wagon. I said, "Yes." I told him of my experience with horses and mules in Arizona, New Mexico, and California. John said, "A man asked for somebody to go after some firewood logs near a mountain. He will pay you." So I worked for a chief of the Yakima Indians. He was very happy to get me. I guess John had told him about me, that I hated to lie around, and that I always helped John and his wife by cutting wood and doing other work around the house. From my young days, I always helped my mother. In Arizona, I worked in the house, cut wood, washed dishes, and took care of my little brothers and sister.

John took me to this man's place. The old Yakima's name was Charley Jobe or Jobe Charley. I believe that he was about fifty years old, and his wife was about thirty-five. I was sorry for Charley Jobe, for he was too old and too sick to do much. His sister had a son about twenty-five years old, but he lived with friends. Living with Charley Jobe was a big man named Jim, a Nez Percé from Idaho, who was married to a niece. Big Jim weighed about three hundred pounds, and he never did any work about the place. He just lay inside and sang all day.

Next morning we left for the timber, which was about twenty miles away near the mountains. I hitched up four horses to a wagon while Charley Jobe and his wife rode in a buggy. They took a teepee along, and we camped three days while I cut timber. The old man asked if I knew how to load the logs, and I told him, "Yes." I cut five long timbers and used a long chain to roll the logs over the wagon wheels. After we got it loaded, we left for home next day.

After that, all I did was chop wood, for there was nothing else to be done. It was snowy, wet, and cold. They had a nice, two-story house, many horses, and big fields, but nothing was ever grown on them. The old chief was very glad to have me at his home. He wanted me to stay and be one of his family. He treated me as though I were a son.

When spring came, they told me about moving to

the Columbia River to fish there, starting about March (1926). I had never seen the Columbia River. They said there was a fishing village along the river, and every year the Yakima Indians went to fish. The government gave them fishing rights for four months. Charley Jobe's nephew lived along the river bank, the only Indian to live there all year around. A lake belonged to him, and his grandfather had left him a fish wheel or two. These fish wheels were revolving scoops which picked up fish and dumped them into a trough, from which they were dropped into a hopper. He had them set on a narrow finger of the river where the wheels caught fishes. As Charley Jobe and his family talked about fishing, I became anxious to see the fishing. Of course, I had already seen salmon in Alaska, but I wanted to see how Indians fished for the salmon.

When the time to go came, I loaded a light wagon. They wanted me to drive it over the mountains just south of Toppenish. They had just bought a little Chevrolet, and Big Jim drove the car. I left in the morning and about dark I was on top of the mountains. There were lots of pine trees up there. One of the horses was wild and mean — kicked all the time. I thought that I'd stop overnight and rest the horses. I tied them to trees, and this mean horse never stayed still; he just went around and around, snorting. I tried to sleep but I could not at this wagon site. About 2 A.M., I looked through the timbers. It was red and looked like a forest fire. I quickly hitched up the horses and started down the other side of the mountains. About daylight I was on the other side and looked again, and there was no fire. In the east the sky was red, like searchlights. When I came down to town, many people were standing in the streets looking at the lights. Nobody knew what they were.

I rested the horses and fed them in the livery stable. Later I crossed the Columbia River on a flat ferry; it cost fifty cents. I rode on about five miles to where they had an Indian village. Next day, when Big Jim and I went to see the horses, one was dead. I was sorry. "I killed him," I said to Jim. "Oh, never mind, he was too old anyhow."

I watched the men fishing with long poles which had dip nets on the end to scoop up the salmon. Some poles had hooks on the end to catch them. Big Jim taught me how to do it, and I caught some. The Indians smoked and dried the salmon. Some were put in barrels and salted. It was interesting to watch the fishing from a little island in the river. There was a cable line from the mainland, and a man would cross in a box. He would sit holding the net over the waterfalls, and a salmon would leap up to reach a place above the falls to lay her eggs. Sometimes the fish would jump right into the net.

I stayed with those people for four months until, at the last of July, they left for their homes on the reservation. Then Charley Jobe's nephew asked me to stay. He lived in a big frame house on the river bank with his sister, Mary, and sometimes her daughter, Juanita, who was Big Jim's wife. I stayed for awhile, and I helped the nephew by watching the fish traps at night. In the morning he would transfer the fish from the trap to a big box, and we would raise it up the steep bank, which was as high as a three-story building. We loaded the fish into a wagon that had sideboards. He would take them to The Dalles to sell, and I used to ride with him.

After he stopped catching salmon on the river, the nephew began to fish on a small lake near his home. We used a row boat to string a line which was five hundred feet long and had hooks every five feet. Two days later we returned to see if anything had got hooked. Nothing. We waited two more days. This time some fish were hooked, but even some three feet long he did not want and threw them back into the lake. I saw that they were a different kind of fish, and I asked him what they looked like. "Sharks," he said, "but they're sturgeon." Later we caught a big one, nine feet long. We tied her to the shore and left her there for several days before he killed her. He was afraid that somebody might see him, because the sturgeon were not allowed to be caught. Anyway, he cut open the belly, took out the eggs (caviar), put them in big cans, and even sold the fish meat.

I stayed with the nephew for three months. I don't remember if he ever paid me anything. Then I left and went back to Toppenish. Sometime later, the nephew and his sister moved to Toppenish to be with Charley Jobe. Charley Jobe had 360 acres of good land, but he didn't farm it. He sold 80 acres, a big frame house and barn, and good fence to a white man for $5,000. I told him, "You sell it kind of cheap." Then he said, "I'm a damn fool. I wish I didn't sell it. It's too late now."

When I was back at Charley Jobe's place, Juanita told me that when she was only thirteen years old she used to live in that frame house on the riverbank with her grandfather. "When grandfather was alive, he owned three fish wheels in the river; he caught many fish." She used to go to town with him to sell the salmon. She would sit on the wagon in town while her grandfather went about. When he returned he would have lots of money with him, and he would give her a dime—no more. Juanita said, "One day, while I was washing dishes, grandfather called me into the next room. He showed me lots of money in a big, square, lard can. He said, 'When I am gone, all of this will be yours.' "

She said, "I was stupid. I was young and did not know about money and didn't care about it. Grandfather told me he was going to hide it in a safe place, but I didn't even look where the old man went." She was sorry and disgusted. She told me that story in 1926. While I was there I didn't think about looking for the money; maybe I was stupid, too. After many years, while I was in Arizona, then I began to think about looking for it, but it was too far away.

It was getting cold again, and I began thinking about Los Angeles and Arizona, where it was warm. Washington sure had a different climate. I waited until spring. By that time I made up my mind to leave. I told the family that I would leave some time to go back home, but I didn't know when. One day it was cold with snow on the ground. The folks did not see me, but I took my suitcase and walked to town and bought a ticket to Seattle. I wanted to see that town before I went on. I stayed three weeks, but I did not try to find a job. It was foggy, cloudy, and rained all the time.

I thought about the fishing villages on the Columbia River, and I wanted to see some of the Indian people. I left Seattle and went to Portland, then to

The Dalles and the Indian village. I was afraid that if I showed up at the village they would not let me leave, so I decided not to get too close. I came back to The Dalles and went on to Portland. I hung around there for a week and then went to Eugene, Oregon. There I found the climate just fine.

I got a job near Klamath Falls, Oregon, doing cement work on a tunnel. I worked two months, got enough money, quit, and went to Los Angeles. Right away I found a job working as a mule skinner near Santa Ana, building a highway. I did not stay long on that job because it was the rainy season; I quit again.

My next job was near Escondido, where a big dam was going up. My job was to shovel gravel into a cement mixer. You had to shovel fast, and nobody could stand that job for very long. Men would come and go; many strong men could not stand that kind of work. I was 5'4" tall and weighed only 135 pounds, but I stuck to the job longer than anyone: I shoveled for about two months. I was thinking about quitting, for it was getting colder and I didn't have any blankets to cover up with. It seemed that the boss read my mind. He came to me and told me to work with the cement finishers. I knew it was an easy job, so I stayed. The job *was* easy. All I had to do was to carry a bucket of cement mix to a man on the side of the big dam. When the cement finisher completed his job, I was paid off.

I decided to go back to Los Angeles to make a little money. It was 1927, and it rained plenty in California. I got to Los Angeles and hung around town spending my money. Many of my tribe were in town, most of them working in different jobs. Some took parts in movies. That's all they did: played Indians, rode horses, and fought play battles. I had tried it once, and it was too cold for me. I did not try to get another job, because I wanted to go to Phoenix, where it was warm. I was tired of rain, fog, and cold. I left California.

I did not stay long in Arizona. I was young and could not stay long in one place, so I decided to go back to Los Angeles. I went to Phoenix, and there I planned to steal rides on a passenger train to Los Angeles. I was getting to be a regular hobo. I had a tough time getting on a train. The yard bulls watched very closely, but I finally got one. Every time it stopped, I got off; when it started up, I jumped on again. The train reached Los Angeles early in the morning, but it was going so fast that I could not jump off until I got to a southern park. Then I walked six miles to the main town.

Right away I found several of the boys I knew. I asked, "Where is Hilare Miguel?" I had heard that Hilare, a Tucson boy, was in Los Angeles. They said, "He works somewhere but he will be here at 5 P.M." He was surprised to see me. That night I stayed with him at his hotel, and more boys came to his room that night. Later he told me, "These boys staying here, they never work. They just try to borrow money from me and everyone all the time. I'm disgusted with them." But he never said anything to them.

One night when we were out in town, he told me that he wanted to get out of Los Angeles and go somewhere. I told him that I had in mind going to Fresno, where I had worked before. I told him that I liked that place and I wanted to leave soon. He said that he wanted to go without letting the loafers know. We did not have much to carry, just a few clothes. This time I paid to ride a bus to Fresno. It was the season when the fruit was ripe and people were starting to pick peaches, apricots, figs, and grapes.

I had been in Fresno before, so they remembered me at the employment office and found us a job picking grapes. They sent us to a place called Clovis, where we had a job working by ourselves. People were camped nearby — hundreds of them. We did not have anything with which to cook, and no blankets. We just slept on the ground. It wasn't cold in the summer. We found some cans to warm things and to make coffee.

One day we noticed that people were still in camp. I asked a man why, and he told me that people had stopped buying grapes. My partner and I went to see our boss. He said that the farmers could not sell their grapes, so they stopped people from picking them. Grapes were just dropping to the ground. But our boss told us to keep picking; we were glad and we did not tell anybody. The place where we were picking was only about thirty acres. When we finished, the man paid us off.

The unemployed people were worried and didn't know what to do. Many had big families and the children were hungry. I was sorry for them, but I could do nothing about it. I told my friend not to show off with his money. We would go out from camp to buy something to eat. We hung around the place for awhile.

One day we talked it over, and we decided to walk to Fresno. While there, we saw a big, strong Papago who had been in Los Angeles and was too lazy to work. He was always trying to borrow money from my friend, and he followed us. We tried to get rid of him, but he stuck to us everywhere. We could not shake him off. We tried to tell him that we were broke and were looking for work. No difference. Our people had nicknamed this man "Sonora." He was a lady's man and a drunkard. Later, in 1967 I saw him at Sells, Arizona, on the Papago reservation. He was a very old man, and he died that year. My sister-in-law told me that he had come to her place and asked to marry her so that he could get all my money! She refused. Finally we lost Sonora in Fresno.

We went back to the Clovis campground, and the people were still there; there was no work, and they didn't have the money to leave. There were Indians from a reservation near Indio there — an old man, his three sons and their wives, and three children of one of the sons. They were nice people. They had old cars, but no gas to go from there to Perris, California, their home. We were sorry for them, for they were all broke. Sometime later, one of the brothers came to us for help. He said that they wanted to get out of there. "Maybe you can buy gas for us to get home." My friend and I talked it over. We finally agreed to buy gas for the two cars, and we left Clovis with them. We went on the coastal highway. Work was scarce everywhere we stopped, and the going was slow. The old cars were overloaded with bedding and twelve people. My friend and I bought bread and other things for them to eat.

We stopped in one town called Oxnard. We spent the night there, and next morning we saw chili pepper plants. A farmer asked us to pick his peppers for ten cents a basket. The job lasted two days, and we got a little money. We tried to find other work around there, but there were no jobs. Finally we got the family to Perris, and the old man wanted us to stay there with them. I was sorry for them, but we couldn't stay; we had to look for jobs for ourselves.

I told the old man that I was going to the Imperial Valley and then to Phoenix. He and his sons had never left their families before, but they wanted to go along because maybe they would find work. He had an old car, a Buick, so one morning we loaded on six of us and left. It was slow going for that old car—it took us all day to get to El Centro. After sundown we found an open space outside of town and slept there. Next morning we drove around, and for three days we tried to find jobs. On the fourth day we found some work cutting milo-maize for $1.50 a day; five of us worked.

In a few days, the old man got a message from home—bad news. He told us that his wife was very sick, and she wanted him to come back home. The father had a talk with his sons. What to do? Then one son asked me to drive the car and take the father home. I did not want to drive back there. I said, "Why don't one of you drive?" But the old man wanted me, so I gave up and told him, "All right, I'll drive." We got ready and left right away.

The car was going all right, but when we got near Coachella Station, it stopped. I did not know the trouble—I was no mechanic. We had gas. I told the old man to help me push the car to a gas station. Maybe the service station man could help us find the trouble.

The man looked at it, but he couldn't tell us what was wrong, and it was getting dark. We left the car at the station and walked about two and a half miles into Indio. We got something to eat and a room.

Next morning we ate breakfast and then walked back to the Coachella gas station. The man had found the trouble, so I paid him and thanked him for his help. We left there and drove to a little place called Perris, the man's home. Sorry to say, his wife did not last long after we got there. I was sorry for the family.

I don't remember how I got back to Brawley, California (just north of El Centro), but I found my friend Hilare Miguel there. We tried hard to find a job, but there was nothing. We hung around Brawley, for we still had a little money left. We found three Papago boys from our reservation who were also hunting for work. My friend asked them where they were staying, and one of them said, "We've got a house in the field." We went over there, and I saw an old ruined frame house—no doors, no windows, and holes everywhere. It had not been lived in for years. He said, "We don't pay rent—it's free!" Those boys had no blankets— they slept on newspapers. That night we all slept on the ground. It was February. One good thing, it never rained.

Each morning the Papago boys got up and went to town. They had nothing to cook. My friend and I still had a little money left, so when the other boys were gone, we went to a store in town and bought a loaf of bread and some canned goods for breakfast. One morning, something happened. While the other boys went somewhere, my friend and I stayed home. I was lying on my back looking at the old frame house with the holes all over, and my friend was walking around outside. I had a feeling that something was hidden somewhere. I got up and walked to the wall where the two-by-fours crossed; I put my little finger behind them and touched something that felt like paper. I worked it out and, at first, I couldn't tell what it was because it was so covered with dirt. I shook the dirt off. It was paper money. It had been there a long time, for the bills were a faded yellow. I counted—there were thirty dollars!

I did not tell my friend. I sure didn't feel good after that, but I knew from the way the money looked that it could not have belonged to the other boys. Still, I was scared. Every day I watched the boys closely to see if they checked where it had been hidden, but they didn't seem to know anything about the money. I did not spend the money for a long time. By then, the boys had gone somewhere; maybe they had found a job.

One morning we went to eat at a little place in town. A man asked, "You boys aren't picking peas this morning?" He said some people were needed just a mile from town. We decided to go because we needed a job. When we arrived, there were hundreds of people there already. I think the field was only about thirty acres. We got our baskets, and each of us took a row. Pretty soon there were fifty or more people on each row, so we quit and went back to town; we had made nothing. That was in 1929.

Later I found a job near El Centro. Two Papagos I knew were there, and they worked for a company which raised everything—watermelons, tomatoes, cantaloupes, lettuce, and cabbage. The company had fields all over in Imperial Valley from Calistoga to Westmoreland. One Sunday morning while I was in an El Centro pool hall watching the boys shoot pool, a man asked me if I knew how to irrigate water-melons, and I said, "Yes." The man came from West-moreland, and he was paying more than I was getting from my company, so I worked nights as an irrigation man. I found some friends in Westmoreland — a Mex-ican named Chico and his half-Papago wife. They asked me to board with them. I did, and I paid them for my eats every week.

One evening in July while I was walking on the railroad tracks, I saw three boys coming my way and laughing about something. When I got close, I saw one of them was my youngest brother, John. I never expected to see him here, because he was never away from Mother or members of our family. At first my brother did not recognize me in the evening light. I asked where they were going, and they said, "We're looking for watermelons. We just arrived last night on freight cars. We want to eat some." I showed them where to find them.

The store nearby had not closed yet. I bought some bread and some canned goods. They were hungry. My brother said that he wanted to go back to Litchfield Park. He told me that Ma and José were all right. Later he told me that José, my oldest brother, had come to Brawley and Calexico looking for me. My sister was very sick, and he wanted me to come home. When he didn't find me, he went home. So, in July 1929, I began to think about my family and to get homesick. I decided to go to Litchfield Park. I told my boss, and he hated to lose me, but he understood.

The Family Man
1929 – 1944

In July 1929 I took a bus from California to Phoenix, and then another to Goodyear, Arizona. From there I walked about a mile to the Goodyear Company's Camp 2. My mother was surprised and very happy to see me. She and my brother José were the only members of the family there, but staying with them was a friend named Emilia Castillo. At first I did not remember Emilia, but then I recalled seeing her picture years ago. Three years before, while I was in Washington State, a Yakima Indian friend had asked to tell my fortune. He read the cards and said, "Oh, you're going to get married. A girl is waiting for you over in Arizona. I see her—a very good woman." I laughed at this prediction because I thought, "I am only thirty-one and too young to get married." Besides, I couldn't support a wife or family, so I soon forgot the prediction.

Emilia was a quiet girl, born in Sonoita, Mexico, which is right on the border and south of our Papago reservation. She was a hard worker at picking cotton and other things. But I had no thought of marriage, even though I was thirty-four. I had a niece named Susie Lawrence, who was married to a colored man, and they lived nearby in another camp. Every time I saw Susie, she kept asking me to marry Emilia. "Please, uncle," she would say. My mother didn't say anything, but she had her ways, too.

Emilia and I were close to one another and, one time, I invited her to go with me to Phoenix for a couple of days. When we returned to the camp, mother and José had moved to another place which they had near Coolidge. Emilia and I continued to live together. This was in 1929. Among the Papago, people may marry early or late. In my day, young for a girl would be sixteen or seventeen, for a boy eighteen or twenty. People generally made their own selection of husband or wife, and the Papagos had no big ceremony for the occasion. They just started living together. Usually the couple established their own home, but, if they could not, they moved into the home of either parent who would accept them.

We decided to move to the Santana District of the Pima reservation, where some of my relatives lived. We thought we would rent a place there. In the Pima reservation there were many Papagos, and many of my relatives were half Papago, half Pima. This inter-mixture went back to the days when the "desert people" used to help harvest the crops of the "river people." Papagos and Pimas speak nearly the same language.

147

When we got to the Pima reservation, a woman let us have fifteen acres of her land which had never been farmed or cleared of mesquite trees. The land was full of big stumps. My brother José and I worked hard cutting trees and pulling stumps to get the land ready. Right away I planted many things — chili peppers, spuds, yams, corn, pumpkins, beans, squash and, of course, watermelons. Our plants grew very good. The agent from Sacaton used to come and admire them. Nobody before ever grew things like that around there. I had learned to raise things at the Santa Fe and Phoenix Indian school farms and while working in California. That year we won several prizes for our vegetables at three fairs — the Arizona State Fair at Phoenix, the Tucson fair, and a fair in Gallup, New Mexico.

When the woman who owned the land saw what we raised, she wanted her land back. She went to the Indian agent at Sacaton and asked for its return. I saw the agent and told him that she had said that we could use the land as long as we wanted and that her husband was too lazy to clear it or to farm it. The agent understood our problem and said that if I gave the land back to the woman, he would help us get started someplace else. We let the woman have her land back, and the agent got me a team of two big mules, harness, plow, and other things for farm work. I was to pay fifty dollars a year for everything. That was a fine arrangement.

An old Pima man — his name was John Louis — heard about me. Before we moved, he came over and asked me to take care of his allotment of forty acres, and his grandson's forty acres. After what had happened, I was doubtful, but the old man begged me to take care of the land. He said, "I am too old to do anything with it and my grandson always works in Phoenix. Besides, he is not fit to work on a farm." The Pima people were good to us, and they helped me to build a little place on John's land. Fifteen men came with wagons to haul posts and gather brush and everything that was needed to make a house Indian-style. My new woman cooked for all, and I helped. We gave them plenty to eat, and everybody was happy.

In the spring people were helping one another on everything — plowing fields and building shacks, and things like that. I was new, so they asked me if I wanted the fields plowed. Everybody wanted to help, and I wanted to get twenty-five acres plowed. Twenty men came with their horses and plows, and the work was finished in a few hours. I was glad for their help, and I thanked them. The next day they helped some-one else.

I planted many things that first year, including cotton seed that I had gotten from the gin near Goodyear. I had a good first crop from that land, and I sold the cotton to the gin owners for a good price. I got to know many people there. We had moved close to Chico Smith, a Papago, and his wife, Lora, and we became good friends. When they had a son born, it was baptised at Bapchule, and my wife and I were his godparents.

The men in our neighborhood liked to play base-ball, both the young and the old. Many players were over thirty, some over forty. At thirty-five, I was still considered young. The captain was a man named López. One day López came over to our place and asked me, "You play ball?" I said, "Yes, a little." He wanted me to play with their new team. I had a good glove and shoes which I always carried with me wherever I went — to China, the Philippines, Alaska, and California. The others had a few, worn-out gloves. We had a meeting to try to collect a few nickels to buy a ball and bat. We were soon playing around the reservation and we even played the prison team in Florence.

Our neighborhood got up a football team, and we played against Sacaton in 1931; I was hurt during the game, but I kept on playing to the end. My side hurt me after the game, but I drove home. That night I could not sleep, and my body was getting stiff. After two days without sleep, my wife asked me to see the medicine man, Manuel Estrella, who lived at Kyren. I knew him well, and I drove over there. He asked me, "What happened?" I told him.

He examined me and said, "Three of your ribs are caved in." He asked me to lie face-down on a cot, and he said, "I hope that you're not ticklish." He reached under my ribs and pulled so quick that it sounded like it cracked my ribs. I jumped up about a foot. He laughed at me and said, "Now get up and run about a hundred yards." It felt good. The next night I could not sleep, so I drove over to tell him. He put his hand where it hurt and applied pressure. The pain stopped. He told me not to work for two weeks, but I was working before the two weeks were over.

Manuel Estrella, the medicine man, was known as far away as California, and people kept coming to him from all over. He was doing a good job of healing diseases which other doctors could not. His patients were soon well. Sometimes we got to visit with those who were coming to see the medicine man. One Papago man who visited us was from Sonoita, Mexico, the same as my wife. He was Abe Estrella, an ex-soldier.

Times were getting hard everywhere. Many people could not make a living farming and the only nearby town, Chandler, was very small and had no work. I did very well on my little farm. The agent often gave me new kinds of seeds to see how good they would do. I planted them and always had a good crop of cotton, beans, squash, wheat, melons, yams, and other things. I was also fortunate to receive a small disability pension of eighteen dollars a month from the Veterans Administration. That was not much, but I thanked God for it. My brother José and my mother moved to Blackwater about the same time as I moved to this land, and their crops were also good.

The wheat I raised my wife ground on a stone to make flour. From our corn we got cornmeal. My wife would skin the pumpkins, cut them in strips, and hang them in the sun to dry; we could keep them for a long time and cook them anytime after that. We also roasted corn to put it away for later, when we would grind it and cook it. Sometimes she boiled the roasted corn until it was about like oatmeal. Then she added bones and boiled some more. The Indians like that. We only had to buy coffee, sugar, and lard. We raised all the other things we cooked.

In 1932 there were no jobs, so the government hired Pima Indians to cut brush for a road toward Casa Grande. I was also hired. Many of the men had no way of getting to work which, eventually, was ten miles away, so I helped them. I volunteered to take some of them in my little Chevy coupe. The job paid no money, but the government gave the men beans, rice, and bacon. Some of the men had big families, and this wasn't enough for them. Some men tried to make a little money by cutting wood, but there was not much mesquite large enough to cut. I was sorry for them — that's why I tried to help transport them, but in time that work gave out. My wife and I were only two, and with our plants and pension, we got along all right.

It was now 1935, and we had no children yet, but we were expecting our first. One day my grandmother's brother, an old man named José Antone, just like my father, came with his Papago woman, named Ceba. Emilia and I did not know that our baby would be born soon. I was outside talking with the old couple when my wife called me. I didn't know what to do, so I ran and called Lora Smith to help my wife. Edward was born that evening, July 29, 1935, and he was baptized at the San Xavier Mission, near Tucson, on September 15, 1935. After our child was born, we were very happy, especially my wife.

During 1935, the irrigation water was getting low, for there was not much water running into the little dam near Sacaton. I would ask for water for my plants, and the waterman would send it, but our place was six or seven miles west of the dam, and the water would not reach me. People in between me and the dam would take the water, and I would get very little or none. My cotton field and my plants were dry, and the harvest was much less. In 1936, it was worse.

The dam pool dried up, and there was no water. My crops died.

We talked it over, and I decided that I would go back to the mine at Ajo. I had worked at the mine before, and I had many friends there. I made a trip to Ajo and talked to a man I knew in the office. He was glad to see me, and I was hired right away, so I went to get my family. We told our neighbors that we were going away, and they were sorry to hear this. A man named José Santo, a councilman, asked me to stay. The council offered me a job as policeman and a small bit of land, but I had already made up my mind to leave. I thought that I had done a good job of fixing up John Louis's land in the five years I had been there. The land was in good condition, except that it was now dry. On Nov. 28, 1936, Emilia, Edward (now fifteen months old), and I left our old place for Ajo.

In Ajo we moved into the Indian village with my cousin, José Johnson, until I found a place to rent in the neighborhood called Mexican town. A few months later I bought a house from a man who was moving to Tucson, and we lived in that house until I left Arizona in 1944. Soon after we arrived, I met Jim Ma-e-tan, Car-me's husband, who worked in the mine.

I was assigned as a shop helper—no more mine pit for me. I liked that work, and they put me at different jobs helping on the engines and trains. My regular job came to be taking care of the locomotive that ran on the company line from Ajo to Gila Bend. I cleaned and oiled the engine each day when it returned to Ajo. The work was not too different from the job which I had done for the Santa Fe Railroad at River-bank in 1923.

In 1938 my health was very poor. People in the mine shop talked about a woman in Escondido, California, who could heal. Many of our people had gone to her for treatment. My family and another family, making eight people, decided to go to her. Mrs. Carline treated people daily and she had a place where people could rent rooms while being treated. However, her treatment did not help any of us.

Dave Holden was my boss at the shop. I was one of two men he picked from the shop to work in the mine well about ten miles north of the Ajo mine. I had never seen a well like that one before. We went eighteen hundred feet down in an elevator, and at the bottom were big rooms. Boiling hot water came from someplace and flowed in four ditches to a big concrete holding tank. Large engines pumped the water to the surface. We were doing some concrete work in the well, and we stayed there all day, each day. It was hot, but very interesting.

One morning, while going down in the elevator, I thought of looking down on one side of the elevator to see the lights at the bottom. The screen fence around the car was four feet high, and I realized that looking down would be dangerous, so I didn't do it. In 1939 the company sent some men down, and one of the men, named Chico, decided to look over the side. When the elevator got to the bottom, the other men saw him lying on the floor dead. His head was busted—almost no head left. Nobody saw it happen in the dark. After this, they fixed the wire cage.

During the Second World War, people in Ajo were afraid that enemy planes might come over and bomb the mines and homes. The Phelps-Dodge Company picked wardens to tell the people what to do in case of an attack. I was selected as warden in Mexican town, where we lived, and Raymond Anita, another Papago, was made warden in the Indian village. There were no attacks during the war.

Many things happened in those years. One windy evening in Ajo, I was at the company store. Someone saw black smoke and hollered, "Fire!" I saw the smoke, ran to my car, and drove to Clarktown, about half a mile away. The Clarktown homes were company houses—frame and very old. The smoke seemed to come from an area where I knew that Papagos lived. Sure enough, it was a friend's home, and the firemen were too late to save it. The strong wind helped the fire, and it was over in a short time. A young Papago pit-mine laborer lived there with his wife and little baby. The wife said that there were people in the house, but there was no chance of rescue.

When the fire was out, they found three bodies, all burned black. Later I asked my friend's wife what had happened. She said that her husband and two friends were drinking. The friends passed out, and later her husband did, too. All lay on the floor. When it got dark, she lit an oil lamp on the little table in the middle of the room. Her husband was lying close, kicked the table, and knocked over the lamp. The fire started. The girl cried out, picked up the little baby, who was lying on the floor, and ran out as fast as she could. Her clothes were burned, and she had no time to get anything or anyone else out. I knew the young man, Pete, and his father. They came from Pisinimo Village on the Papago reservation. He had not been married very long and this was their first baby.

Our people were getting worse from drinking wine and tequila. Some of our boys were bringing a lot of tequila across the border from Sonoita, Mexico — more than they were allowed by the regulations. Some crossed the mountains into Mexico on horseback. No matter what, they always found a way to get it. It was not only a problem for the Indians; the company was losing money because the men got drunk and couldn't work. The company wanted to do something about the heavy drinking so as to keep the men on their jobs.

One day the superintendent called me to his office and asked me to be a police deputy. I did not want the job, but he wanted me to take it real bad. I guess that he knew that in the Army I was sometimes on military police, and that I did not drink. I took the job. I was told to pick someone to work with me, so I selected Ciprano Ocheo, a big man who also worked in the shop. Soon a man came to teach us what a policeman should do, especially if there was trouble. We worked very closely with the superintendent, the Ajo police, the border patrol, and sometimes the F.B.I.

We patrolled Mexican town and Indian village during the nights. We watched for Papagos drinking and for drunks. We told the men to go home and sleep so that they could work the next day. If we caught the same man drinking again, we put him in jail overnight. In the morning we told him to go to work. If he didn't, we fined him ten dollars. Every ten days, I reported to the superintendent. He was glad that we did a good job of getting the men to work, and the men were happier in the pit mine.

Once in a while the F.B.I. would send a man looking for a draft dodger on the reservation. They came to me because I knew the reservation very well. The border patrol sometimes came to learn about the people who were bringing tequila across the border to Ajo. Often these border-crossers were friends of mine, and I hated to tell the border patrol. Also, I disliked having to arrest my own friends. All of my friends drank tequila, and I had too much feeling for them. I liked my job, but, at the same time, I did not feel very good. My wife understood this, and she tried to help all she could. Sometimes I felt very bad and had pain inside my eyes and head. I got to where I could not read a newspaper. One day I told my wife that I would like to go away somewhere for a change.

We now had two boys. Edward was seven and not yet going to school. Joseph had been born in Ajo on March 15, 1938, and was now four. I stayed with the job until 1944, doing the best job of deputy that I could. Everything seemed normal again; the men were not drinking so much, so we did not have to chase them so much. But it was always night work, and, when we were not in our areas, we often had to help the police in Ajo. Still, I wanted to quit. I told Ciprano, and I hoped that maybe someone else would want the job. I went to see our chief and told him that I wanted to quit the police job. He said, "Why do you want to quit?" I explained to him that I was not feeling well. He did not believe me and said, "You look strong and healthy." Then he told me to talk to the superintendent.

The superintendent was a very good man. When I went to him, he said, "What do you want to tell me?" I said, "Bad news. I talked with my chief about quitting my job, and he sent me to talk to you." The superintendent was surprised; he looked at me for a long time and then said, "You look well and strong." I tried to tell him how I felt. He said, "I hate to let you go. You have done a good job for the company. I want you to go have the doctor examine you and find out what is the problem."

The doctor at the company hospital told me that there was nothing wrong with me. He said, "Go back to work. If you leave, you won't get a certificate, and without it you won't get a job anywhere." I was mad, but I said nothing and left the hospital. I said to myself, "I'll show you that I can get a job wherever I go." That evening, after the doctor's examination, I turned in my badge and everything to my chief. He was sorry to see me go away.

I told our tribal leader, Joe Blaine, that I was leaving Ajo. My family had already packed our things with some help from our friends. We sold our house in Mexican town, and we sold or gave away the things we could not carry. We said goodbye to our many friends. Then we drove to the San Xavier Reservation, near Tucson, where my mother and brothers were now living.

My wife, Emilia, was a Catholic, and she had always wanted a church wedding. On June 4, 1944, in the San José Mission Station, operated by the San Xavier Mission, we were married by Father Nicholas Perschl. Before the wedding, Emilia was baptized. Juan and Mary Ortega, our friends, were the witnesses. Emilia was very happy. A few days later we left Tucson for California. I told my folks that we would be near Long Beach or maybe San Pedro. We were on our way.

Faith and Healing

1944 – 1957

After we left the San Xavier Reservation in July, 1944, we drove to Wilmington, California, where we found a place to camp in a vacant lot. A Mexican family was living nearby, and they came to see us. The husband told me where I could find the employment office. When I went there next day, I found many people waiting. It took a long time for my turn to come. The employment people asked me if I was a veteran and where I came from. Then they asked me where I lived. I told them that I had just come to California and that I was camped under a tree on a vacant lot. They called someone and told me where to find a trailer court outside of Torrance. Luckily, the Luime Park Trailer Court was the same one where my cousin, Elmer Molino, lived with his wife and children. He asked us to stay with his family until I found a job. Our older son began going to the Gardena Elementary School.

At the agency I was told that there wasn't much work around, but to come back the next day. When I returned, the employment office gave me a note to go to the Goodyear rubber plant. Elmer showed me where it was—about half a mile from the trailer court. When I was hired for the job, I thought about what the doctor in Ajo had said; I wished that he could see me working so soon.

My new boss asked me if I had ever worked in a rubber plant. I said, "No, I've never seen how rubber is made." He took me around. From a railroad boxcar, men unloaded big sacks filled with what looked like cement or soap. The unloaders opened the sacks and poured them down a big opening. Ninety-pound blocks of rubber came out of the other end of the line. When the rubber blocks came out, four men loaded them on little carts and then put them in stacks six feet high. This was what I was asked to do. At first the work was not so heavy, but the lifting began to get to me. I was new, but I had done heavy work before in the Ajo mine, and I was able to keep up with the other men.

I liked that job all right, and I got along fine with the men and the boss. The boss seemed to like my work; he said, "You are a good worker; you work all the time." After several months I began to feel my shoulder bothering me, and it kept getting worse. When I got home, my wife would rub Vicks on my back, but it didn't seem to do any good. Finally, my wife asked me to quit this job of heavy lifting. I told the boss that I had hurt my shoulder in the mine in Arizona some time ago. The boss wanted to keep me, and he was sorry to see me quit. I was sorry myself.

Because of the pain in my shoulder, I could not sleep nights. After that, I do not know what happened. My wife told me that I just lay on the bed and never said anything, as if I were sleeping all the time. When I didn't eat, she poured orange juice in my mouth. I lay there almost a month. My wife was worried, but she spoke no English, and she didn't ask anyone for help. She nursed me and made me well.

After a month in bed, I suddenly got up and had no feeling of pain in my shoulder. I did not know that I had been laid up that long. Then I remembered that I had not received my pay from the rubber plant. I drove over there. The boss was surprised to see me and he asked me to stay. "No," I said, "I am still weak after a month in bed." My wife and I talked it over and decided that I should take it easy before I tried for another job.

My next job was at a factory making artillery shell casings. Some men who lived at the trailer court worked at a brass foundry, and they told me to go there and ask for a job, so I did. The boss asked me if I had ever worked in a foundry. I told him, "No." The boss showed me the cooking pots where the brass was melted. A man with thick gloves carried a big dipper. Another man poured the red-hot brass into the dipper, and then the man with the dipper carried it to a machine that was turning. The machine was making shell casings for the Army. After I was trained, I ran the machine while the men poured the hot copper in it. It was a hot job in a hot place. This job did not last long. The Army contract for making shell casings ended, so the foundry closed in 1945 and laid off all the men.

When I started looking for another job, I went to the Longry Aircraft Company in Torrance. It was a small plant not far from our home. I had never worked in an aircraft factory. A lady in the plant office was the boss. She asked many questions. I told her that I had just been laid off at the brass factory. She knew all about that. She wanted to know all about my record, for I might be a spy.

I was hired in a couple of days, and I began to work from 4 P.M. to 1 A.M. There were many people there—more women than men. At first I carried armor plates to heat them. Later I was given a job as a saw-man, cutting steel plates for airplanes. I got along just fine with everybody, and they were very nice and friendly, especially after they learned that I was a Papago Indian from Arizona. But that job did not last very long, either. They laid off all the people, and the factory closed.

I decided to take my family back to the San Xavier Reservation for a visit with my mother, La-Lee, and my two brothers. Then I left my family in Arizona and I returned to California. When the aircraft plant had closed, the boss had given me a slip of paper. It said I was to go see a small machine shop in Gardena which needed men. I had decided to try to get a job in the shipyards, and I applied at the Consolidated Steel Corporation. I went to the office and asked for work. They asked me whether I was a veteran and I told them that I was. They signed me up and sent me to the doctor, who said I was all right to go to work. I was told to come back the next day and start as a pipe fitter's assistant.

While my family was in Arizona, all of the people

in the Luime Park Trailer Court were told to move to Banning Homes, near San Pedro. We were assigned to 1008 Rubicon Court. This was a better place, and we had more room. However, both the husband and wife were required to sign the lease. For awhile I didn't know what to do, but then the family surprised me by arriving back in California in time for my wife to sign for our place. I had to take our boys out of the Gardena School and enroll them in the 15th Street Elementary School in San Pedro. The Consolidated Steel Company shipyard was about a mile away, and I soon had four men riding to work with me in my Studebaker.

Although the doctor said that I was all right, I began again to have trouble with my shoulder, back, legs, chest, and head. Sometimes I coughed. My left leg was kind of paralyzed and so was my left arm. Just the same, I worked all the time, and I handled the pipes and tools all right. A friend saw that I looked weak, and he said that I ought to see a doctor. I told him that I was all right. Later, I told him that I got the cough from the Germans overseas. "Oh, you've been gassed," he said. I told him that I was twice in the hospital in France and that I had been wounded as well.

In Banning Homes we lived next door to the Harry Gunnersen family—a man, his wife, and crippled daughter. They came to California for their health from back east in Minnesota. They were all very well now. Mr. Gunnersen had come from Norway, and he was a very friendly man. Each evening he seemed to be waiting for me, and he stood on the porch near the steps. He knew that I didn't want to talk, but he would say, "Hi," and I would say, "Hi" back and go inside. I felt pain all over and just wanted to lie down. No one could seem to do anything about it.

Every day this man was standing in the same place. One day, after coming home from work, I was feeling a little better, so I thought I would talk to him and get to know our neighbor. I knew that he wanted to talk to me. He asked me about my job and whether I liked it. "Yes, I like to work there." Then he asked me about my family and where we came from. I told him. After that I stopped and talked to him a few minutes every day.

One day when I came home from work, he said, "You seem to be in pain." I said, "Yes, I have had a lot of pain for a long time but I have kept on working. I have a family." He asked, "Have you tried doctors?" "Yes, many of them, but they cannot do anything about it. I have also tried all kinds of medicine."

Another evening he told me the story of himself and his family. He owned some kind of construction company. He became sick, and later, so did his whole family—wife, daughter, and two sons. He said, "Now we are all well, except that my daughter can't walk." I did not ask him how he got well. I didn't want to ask too much at one time. All along he knew my trouble, but he did not ask me. Later, I told my wife that Mr. Gunnersen seemed to know things about life that we did not know. Maybe I could learn something from him if I listened. Now and then, I would let him talk to me whenever I had time.

He asked our family to visit them in their apartment. My wife could not speak English, so she would make signs and I would try to explain to her what they said. The Gunnersens wanted to know about our people on the reservation. I told them that there are three Papago reservations, that our people are poor, and that they live in the desert of Southern Arizona. "Nowadays," I said, "we are scattered all over in many states."

One evening in his apartment, Mr. Gunnersen told me about his sickness in Minnesota. Every one of his family seemed to have the same kind of trouble. Then he went to a practitioner that a lady told him about. She treated him and, later, the whole family. When his family came to California, he studied a little book the practitioner had given him. He showed me a little black book. It was called *Eschatology: The William Walter Method*. He wanted to lend it to me.

I told him that I didn't know many words in English . . . like "eschatology." He told me that it was about that part of religion concerned with things like death, judgment, heaven, and hell. He said, "Reading this book will make you learn." So I took the little book. As soon as I got inside, I started to read it as best I could. The first night I read and skipped many words I didn't know. I just knew small words.

The next day I told Mr. Gunnersen that I would bring the book back. The words were too hard for me to understand. He said, "You keep the book and read it a little bit every day." I read it only after supper, but, after a few nights, I became very interested. I would read one page over and over. Every time I read it, it seemed to me that new words were coming out and that I stayed in one place. I told Mr. Gunnersen what I was doing, and he laughed and said, "You are learning. Keep it up."

I told Mr. Gunnersen that I would like to buy a copy of Mr. Walter's book. He said, "I can get one for you in Los Angeles." That Saturday we drove to Los Angeles to look for William Walter's book. We looked in many stores. It was hard to find a copy. We finally found one of his books, called *The Pastor's Son*, a story about a son who was about to die. While walking on the street, the boy found a book on Christian Science and studied it in his room without letting his parents know. He healed himself.

Walter's method was easy to understand, and I liked it. I would read every night, sometimes until midnight or even 2 A.M. While I was reading, I would forget my troubles. Each afternoon as I returned home, I would meet Mr. Gunnersen. He would ask me about my work and talk of many things, but he never asked me how I was doing on my reading. I began to feel much better. Maybe reading and studying the book and believing it helped. I sure wanted to get well, and I tried hard to understand. I did not tell Mr. Gunnersen what I felt, but I kept reading and trying to know all the hard words.

After studying for two months, one night I came home anxious to begin my reading. After supper I lay down, as I always did. Suddenly I went to sleep with the book lying on my chest. During the sleep something strange happened. My bed seemed to go around very fast. I thought that I was holding onto the sides of my bed while it was going around like a windmill. I was scared. When I woke up I was still scared, but I was not holding onto the sides of the bed at all.

Next morning I went to work as usual. I thought, "I'll tell Mr. Gunnersen what happened to me last night." That evening I told him. He laughed and said, "I did not tell you that this might happen, for I did not expect it so soon. Don't be afraid. It may happen to you again." Later he told me why it happened: because I was beginning to learn God's truth, I was beginning to understand what I had read. He said that from my reading, I was being purified of my sins. I could not understand that, even though he tried to explain it.

As I said, my left arm and leg were weak and partly paralyzed. I usually moved very slowly when I was asked to get something for the pipe fitter. Several days after my experience, the pipe fitter asked me to get a piece of iron about two feet long from the scrap-iron pile five hundred feet away. While I was walking and not paying much attention, it was almost as if I went to sleep. When I came to, I was walking very fast. As I walked, it was almost as if I were not touching the ground. I stopped and looked at my leg and arm to see if anything had changed. I felt so good that I almost jumped for joy.

I picked up the iron and walked back to the ship and climbed up the ladder as high as a three-story building. I guess that I went very fast, for everybody noticed me. One friend said, "Look at Chief (my nickname there). Look how fast he goes up and down that ladder. It must be quitting time." He was joking, but he didn't know how good I felt after many years of trouble. I didn't tell him because he would not believe me.

I could hardly wait to tell Mr. Gunnersen and my family. I got home about 4:30 P.M. Mr. Gunnersen was not standing on the porch to welcome me as he usually did. I guessed that he had gone to Long Beach where he often talked in a park with old people and the sick and crippled. In the house I felt very good. I kept on walking around the room instead of lying down as I usually did. My wife did not seem to notice. I asked her if she noticed a difference in my walk. "Oh, your leg. What happened?" she asked. I said, "I am well and walk good. Also my arm is strong now, my whole body feels good."

My wife was not feeling very good herself. She had had female trouble ever since the last baby was born in 1938. She saw many doctors in Arizona and California, but they did no good. One day I talked to my wife about a treatment for her. I asked Mr. Gunnersen if he knew a practitioner, and he said, "Yes, in Los Angeles." He made an appointment and on that day we went to see Rose Pardner Martindale. This was in December 1945. I explained to the practitioner about my wife's trouble. She asked me if I understood about the science of eschatology. I told her, "No, I only started reading the book Mr. Gunnersen lent me." Then she asked me my religion. I said, "I am supposed to be Catholic, but I have not gone to church for many years." I also told her that Mr. Gunnersen had explained to me about eschatology, but that my wife had not had it explained to her. Mrs. Martindale said that she would treat my wife from her home. She sent a note to explain to my wife what to do, and I explained it to Emilia. In a week, she felt fine, and she never had any further trouble. I thanked Mrs. Martindale for her help.

From then on, I studied the Walter method during all my spare time at home and at work. I could climb like a monkey, and the men often called me that. Mr. Gunnersen used to say, "When you know the truth, nothing can harm you." I had in mind all the time that nothing could hurt me.

One day the boss asked me to climb up on a big pipe which was about thirty inches around and fifteen feet up. I was to tighten the big nuts all around a fitting. I got up on the pipe, lost my balance, and started to fall backward. I saw a little pipe above me and I grabbed it with both hands. It was a hot steam pipe and my hands stuck to the pipe, but I got them loose and fell to the floor. Everyone came running to see if I was hurt. I told them that I wasn't hurt, but I did not want to look at my hands. The skin was burned and all dried up. I climbed up again, tightened the bolts, and forgot all about it. When I got home, I told my wife what had happened. She took a look at my hands. To our surprise, they were not burned— they were just as good as before. My wife laughed at me.

Another time I was helping a welder when a three-inch pipe, about three feet long, was dropped by one of the men about three stories up. It hit me across the shoulder. The men close to me were scared. They ran to where I was sitting and asked me if I was hurt. I said that I felt something hit me, but I paid no attention. I kept on working, and a friend said, "You must be made of iron. You don't have a scratch." I didn't tell him why, because I hadn't learned much about the science, and I didn't know how to explain it.

In May of 1946, the Consolidated Steel Corporation finished its last ship and was closing. I was one of the last men they let go. Then I signed up to work at the Todd Shipyard as a jackhammer man, but after three months they also closed. Work was getting scarce. Men who had no jobs were hanging around the union office. Several times I went there, but they had no jobs.

Across the San Pedro Bay was the Bethlehem Steel Company's ship-repair yard. I went there and asked for a job. They asked me a few questions, and I was hired in November 1946. Work began to slow down there. They laid off some men, and they cut the work week to three days. Even though there was not much work available, I decided to quit that job and look for another one.

I did not want to return to Arizona at that time, for I liked California, and we had many friends in San Pedro. I was going to the Christian Science Church, and our two sons were going to Sunday School. Everyone was in good health. I told the family that I did not want to look for a job just yet. I said that maybe we could go out for a drive and see the country. Right away my wife said, "Why don't we go to Hemet and pick apricots?" She had seen this little town on one of our drives from Los Angeles. I agreed that we'd go there and maybe stay two weeks.

On the first of July 1947, we drove to Hemet and we hoped that we'd see some of our people there. I drove through the apricot orchards, and we saw many people, mostly Mexicans, camped under the trees waiting for the apricots to ripen. I stopped at one farmer's house and asked when the picking would begin. He said, "In a few days. If you folks want to pick, I'd be glad to have you pick for me. There are three army tents. You can move into one." Another tent was used by three young Mexican boys. This farmer, Mr. Mineral Walm, was about twenty-eight years old, and he had a young wife and a baby daughter. They were nice people.

Mr. Walm and three Mexican boys did all the picking, while I kept track of the number of trays each of the boys picked, and I brought the apricots to a central place. My wife cut the apricots in half, took out the seeds, and put the halves in trays. A man put the trays on the ground to dry. We all got along fine.

Our sons were regular apricot eaters. Their faces were covered with apricots. They climbed the trees, ate apricots, and wanted no dinner. After work one evening, I was sitting outside our tent reading my book. My wife was working inside, and the boys were climbing the trees. I began to feel dizzy and felt that something was happening. Later Mr. Walm told us that there had been an earthquake and that it knocked things from his walls.

One afternoon while I was checking trays, a Mexican boy named Alberto came to me and said that Mr. Walm had fallen from his fifteen-foot ladder. When he hit the ground he doubled up like a jackknife. One of the boys turned him on his back. Then they took him home. After work, I went to see Mr. Walm. He was in great pain, and he could not lie still. His wife was upset and did not know what to do. I asked her if she knew anyone who could help him, and she said,

"No." I was very sorry for him, and I was praying silently.

I told Mrs. Walm that I studied Christian Science and, while I was new, I would try my best to help him with my prayers. I told her to tell Mr. Walm that at 8 P.M. I would be praying for him and for him to think about it. Then I left for my tent. I memorized some short prayers and at 8 P.M. I sat in a dark tent praying for one hour. I went to sleep thinking that in the morning everything would be all right.

In the morning the boys were up early climbing in the trees. My younger son, Joe, came in the tent and woke me. He said, "Daddy, I see Mr. Walm out there spreading trays." I asked him, "Are you sure it's him?" "Yes, it's him." I wanted to be certain, so I got up and dressed. I did not want him to think I was spying, so I went behind the tent and watched. It sure was him. I could hardly believe that my prayers had helped in so short a time. I did not say anything about it but just went to work.

The next day I saw Mrs. Walm. She was very happy that her husband was well, and she thanked me for helping. Before the accident, I was not sure that my prayers would help. Mr. Gunnersen used to say that some people would study for years and could not heal the sick. Others learned quickly.

One of the Mexican boys asked me how Mr. Walm got well so quickly. I told him that I prayed for him. Then Alberto said that he would like to learn to cure people. The boys spoke very little English, and I told them that I would try to find them a book written in Spanish; maybe I could find it in Calexico. Alberto asked me to come visit him in Mesilla, Mexico, whenever I came that way.

One day Alberto was very sick. He asked for me to come see him. I went to his tent, and he was in bed covered with heavy blankets. Still he was cold, shaking, and had a high fever. He told me that he wanted to go home but that he had very little money. He asked me to help him — "Like you helped Mr. Walm." I told him that I would pray for him right away. "Don't worry, but think about me praying for you."

I returned to my tent and told my family that I would pray for Alberto. I took out my little notebook in which I wrote some prayers for treatment. That evening I prayed for him for an hour. Before I went to bed, I went to see him. He was feeling fine. His fever was gone, but he was still in bed as I had told him. He was smiling, and I knew he was all right. I asked him, "You still want to go home?" He smiled and said, "No, I'll stay and work." He was happy. Next morning he was at work again.

When the apricot picking was about over, I told Mr. Walm that we were going back to San Pedro, where we lived. He asked us to come back and work for him again. When we were leaving, he gave us a big box full of dried, cured apricots, and a box of fresh peaches. We said goodbye and left Hemet for San Pedro.

Back at San Pedro, jobs were scarce. The employment office was always crowded, and they could offer me nothing. The union couldn't find us work, but we still had to pay our dues. I thought of going back to Tucson. I told Mrs. West, the adult Sunday school superintendent, that I had no work and that we might have to go to Arizona. She said, "There's work for you everywhere. You can get a job anyplace." Then she asked me where I wanted to work. I said, "I'd like to get a job at the Navy shipyard." She read some works in the Bible and talked to me about God. At that time I knew very little about Christian Science because it was too hard for me to understand. She told me to go to the shipyard and ask for a job.

I did not go until the next day, for it was already late. At the main office there were many men in the hall looking for jobs. A lady asked me what I wanted. I said, "I want work," but she told me that they weren't hiring. Another lady who was sitting near heard me talk. She called me inside and asked me a few questions: "Where are you from? What do you do? Are you a veteran?" After I answered, she gave me a form to be filled out and returned in two days. I thanked her and went home. I went again to see Mrs. West to let her know that I had gotten a form. She was very happy that her prayers worked. Mrs. West helped me to fill out the papers.

When I returned to the shipyard, the lady at the office asked me if I was a graduate. I told her, "No." "You just learned the machine-shop work at the mine?" "Yes, as a helper on a locomotive and other machines." I was hired, and that night I told my family that we were not going back to Arizona yet.

I started to work in the Navy shipyard at Long Beach on Terminal Island in 1947. When a ship came in for repair, my crew worked on the machinery and propeller shafts. I had never been inside a warship before. I worked on many kinds of ships — battleships, cruisers, destroyers, aircraft carriers, landing craft, and others. Sometimes I worked during the days, sometimes at night.

One night I was working on a propeller shaft, four or five floors down. I did not come up because it was too high to go to the top just to eat lunch. I thought that I was alone. After eating, I walked to another part of the ship. There I saw a colored man sitting with his hands over his face. When he heard me, he moved. I could see that something was wrong. I asked him, "Why are you down here?" He said, "I cannot see." I asked him what happened. He said, "When I came to work, I was all right. My eyes were a little sore, but I could see all right. Now I don't know what to do." His eyes were closed; he could not open them.

I asked him, "Mind if I help?" "No," he said, so I put my fingers on his eyes for about ten minutes and prayed as best I could. When I took my fingers away, he was afraid to open them. It had hurt when he tried before. I told him not to be afraid. He opened them, and he was surprised. He thanked me for my help. "I don't know what I'd have done if it wasn't for you. You found me and now my eyes feel very good." He wanted to get to know me better.

Another time we were working in a machine shop aboard a ship. Another machinist, a colored man named Jim Jolley, worked with us. He came in late one night wearing a heavy overcoat and had his face all wrapped up. He could not talk, just whistle. But he went about his job without complaint. Our lunch time was at midnight. I asked him if he had a sore throat. He shook his head, "Yes." I told him that I would try to help him if he wished. "All right." We went behind a machine. I could see that his neck and face were swollen. I put my fingers on his throat for minutes while praying. When I took my fingers away, he felt himself and smiled. He felt fine, and he could talk. He thanked me and went to his work on the machines.

Jim Jolley lived in Los Angeles and was a part-time tailor. He was so happy to feel well that he asked to make me a suit. I told him that what I had done was for him because he was sick. I told him I wanted nothing. I was glad to have learned how to treat people with prayer and I helped everyone I could. From that time on, I helped many people—most of them colored. These men seemed easier to heal than others. They had faith in the Bible.

My machinist boss was a tall man named Johnson, a very good man. He put me to helping the first-class machinist who did the most important jobs. I got along fine with this man. He seemed to like my work. Then I received a note from the sergeant of the security guard asking me to see him in his office. I guess he knew that I had been an M.P. in the army and a deputy in Ajo. He wanted me to transfer to the security force, but I wanted to stay as a machinist.

In 1950, our work was slowing down. There was very little work on the ships. The men knew that the shipyard might close, and our boss told us that it would be soon. A notice was then placed on the bulletin board telling each man when he would check out. I was glad to learn that I would stay until the last—April 17, 1950. Before we left, each man was asked if he wished to transfer. I was asked to go to Port Hueneme Seabee Training Base. Someone suggested that I ask for the Naval Air Base at Litchfield Park, in Arizona, so that I would be close to home. But I told them that I wanted to go home to the San Xavier Reservation near Tucson. On the day of leaving, each of us had to check out our tools to be sure that we did not steal any government property.

It took nine days for my family to pack and ship our things. We waited until the last of the month before we left. At the Dana Junior High School they were sorry to see Edward leave, and at the 15th Street Elementary School, the principal was especially sorry to lose Joe, for he was the only Indian in their school. It was hard to leave all of the friends we had made in seven years. There were the Gunnersens, who showed me God's truth and the science of healing. Mrs. Kuyriles, superintendent of the boys' Christian Science Sunday school, came to say goodbye. There were many more.

My mother was surprised when we arrived at the San Xavier Reservation, for I had not told her that we were coming home. After we got settled, I went to see Mrs. Schuck, superintendent of the Sunnyside School District, and asked to enroll Edward and Joseph. I told her about their schooling in California, and she was interested in them. She said that they had no Indians in their schools. The next day I took the boys and signed them up. Everything was just fine. The boys had to walk over three miles each day along a brush trail to reach their school. The junior high school that Edward attended in 1950 was a small, gray, two-story building. Joe's elementary school was a long building. When Edward finished junior high in 1952, Sunnyside had no high school, so he went to Tucson High School. It was large and a real change for him.

I did not try to find a job at first but decided to build us a little shack. I thought that if I built my home near the Nogales Highway, the boys would be closer to school—only half a mile away. It did not take long to build it. One day my sister-in-law, Fernando's wife, came to our new house and asked me if I wanted to work. Her boss, Mary Pennington, ran the Geronimo Hotel near the University, and she wanted to talk with me. I told Mrs. Pennington that I had never worked in a hotel before, but they knew that I had had many experiences at the Indian schools, the Montezuma Sanitarium, and at the shipyard. Mrs. Pennington's son, Neal, was a Navy veteran, and he wanted me to help with both cleaning and maintenance. All of the Penningtons—Mrs. Mary; her daughter, Catherine; Neal and his wife, Hazel—were nice people.

Every morning I caught the bus near the Nogales Highway, and I rode the bus home in the afternoon. I didn't drive my old car to work. In addition to the Penningtons, there were four maids—two whites and two Indians. Mr. Pennington showed me my job. Every morning I was to clean the hallways and lobbies first, then do whatever maintenance work the boss wanted: fix showers, toilets, sinks, furniture—or maybe do some painting. I did a little of everything. When Mr. Pennington saw that I could fix things, he did not hire men to do this work anymore. I even helped him work on a big heater-cooler system.

The Penningtons introduced me to the people who lived in the hotel. Most of them seemed to be very friendly and, in time, I got to know them very well. Nearly everyone came from back East—I guess for health reasons. Some came in the fall and left in the spring; others liked the climate and didn't go back but stayed for good.

No one at the hotel knew that I went to the Christian Science Church or that the boys went there to Sunday School. The boys stopped going, and I eventually stopped also. I continued to study the Walter method at home and sometimes when I was not busy at work. I found that some of the people at the hotel were Christian Scientists, but they did not know how to heal themselves. Some of these people had studied *Science and Health* for a long time, but they were still sick. I learned this because I talked with them, but I never told them that I knew a little about Christian Science.

The hotel had a basement where they kept beds, chairs, and other things. I ate my lunch down there every day because it was cool in the summer and warm in the winter. One day Miss Pennington came down to switch on the heat, and she caught me reading my little booklet. She asked me what I was reading, and I told her that I was reading the Walter method so I would keep in good health. I guess she told her mother.

Several months later, Miss Pennington did not show up for work even though it was her turn to be in the office. I was surprised because she never missed work. Her mother came in her place and I asked her, "Where is Catherine?" Her mother said that she did not feel well so she stayed in bed. Then Mrs. Pennington asked me to pray for her. I told her that I would think about her now but that when I was at home, in a quiet place, I would pray at 8 P.M. "You tell her to think of me praying for her at that time." When the time came, I prayed as best I could the little prayers that I had learned. I prayed for one hour.

Next morning I came to work at the hotel, and I was surprised to see Miss Pennington in the office doing some paper work. Only joking, I said, "I did not expect to see you today here in the Hotel Geronimo." She laughed and told me what happened. "Mama told me, 'Jim (everybody at the hotel called me Jim) will pray for you at 8 P.M.' I was sleeping and this morning I just got up, dressed, ate breakfast, and came to work. I forgot that I had been sick. Mama did not want me to come to work, but I told her that I felt just fine."

I worked every day, inside and out, fixing things, painting the walls, and cutting the lawn. One day there was plumbing trouble in several rooms. Mrs. Pennington asked me to see what was wrong, so I went to one of the rooms, and I saw that the toilet bowl was overflowing. Then the maid called me to Room 20, where the toilet was running over on the floor. Miss Matthew was in bed sick, but I did not notice her. I had missed her for some time, but I thought that she had probably gone away. I went to dipping water with a bucket and emptying it outdoors. Then I saw Miss Matthew. Her face was very white, and she did not say anything. Finally she told me that she had been lying there in bed for two weeks. I did not know what to do. I went to look at the next room; then the maid called me back to Room 20. The water was running on the floor again. At the same time, Miss Matthew wanted to talk with me. "About what?" I thought. She asked me to sit down, but I had to dip water and throw it out every minute.

I asked, "You want to talk with me?" "Yes," she said. "Somebody told me that you know how to pray, and I want you to pray for me. I am tired of lying in bed sick." I told her that I would be back soon. I went down to the basement to get my little prayer book. I copied some prayers and came back to read them to her:

> You are the image and likeness of God; you live and have your being in God. Therefore you are perfect. You can be nothing else than perfect because you live, move, and have your being in God in perfection . . .

When the water started to run over again, I stopped my prayers, started to dip water, emptied it, sat down . . .

> . . . and you could not be anything else. It is not possible and this belief of error which you have, which we term fever, is not real but, on the contrary, it is transitory. It is not true. Not real . . .

I read again, then emptied again.

> . . . simply a mental belief and a person who has, or

thinks like this, when confronted with the truth is annihilated. We here and now deny its reality and denounce it as error and false, and declare that all that is, is God manifest. All that is, is good, is harmony. This error called fever, is unreal, untrue, and does not exist and cannot exist in reality because it is a lie, because it denies the allness of God and the allness of good.*

I was there about thirty minutes working and praying. When I looked at Miss Matthew, her face began to get red. She asked me if it was all right to sit up and get dressed. I said, "If you want to." She got dressed and walked around the room smiling. Then she said, "Tomorrow I am going to work." She worked at an office in town. Next morning when I came to work, she was on the corner waiting for a ride. This woman never thanked me for helping her.

One evening when I had just gotten home from work, I sat down to eat supper. I heard an airplane coming very close — it sounded like it would hit our house. We lived west of the airport, and we often heard airplanes approaching, but not like this. I ran out the door just in time to see a big plane hit the high voltage wires near our place. The plane slid over the Nogales Highway and bounced over a fence. I forgot all about my supper and ran toward the crash.

The sun was down, and I did not see a cable which the airplane had cut. It was across my path. The cable

---

*William W. Walter, *The Pastor's Son*, rev. ed. (Aurora, Illinois: by the author, 1908).

caught me by the neck, and I was thrown to the ground. I got up shaken, and I walked to the crash. Men were jumping out of the plane. Someone inside had chopped a hole, and the men tumbled out. The plane began to burn and soon went up like Fourth of July fireworks.

The noise of the plane crash brought many people to see what had happened. I told them about the crash and how the broken wire had caused my fall. One man said, "You're lucky. You ought to be thankful you are alive." The electric wire was dead.

I left the Geronimo hotel in 1957 after thinking about it for a long time. The Penningtons had been so nice to me that it was very hard for me to tell them. I told the maids. They were the same ones who had been there when I came. One afternoon when Mr. Pennington was in the office, I told him that I wanted to quit my job. He was surprised. He asked me, "Why? Is something wrong or someone mad at you?" I said, "No, I am planning on building a home on my land allotment. I am going to retire." The Penningtons were very disappointed, and I hated to leave the hotel.

The Retirement Years
1957 Onward

The years in Tucson passed very pleasantly. We had our own house south of town, even if it wasn't much. Each day the boys left for school, and I went to work. Emilia was always busy at home. Sometimes she worried about being left alone, but it was always all right. The boys were enrolled in Sunnyside Elementary and then Sunnyside Junior High School. When they finished there, they went to Tucson High School. Joe, my second boy, played baseball and football on his school's teams. In 1950 Edward joined the Air Scouts and, with the other boys, built things to show. During the Scout-o-Rama, Ed explained about airplanes to many people.

Ed was picked in 1951 to go to the Philmont Scout Ranch in Cimarron, New Mexico. There were lots of mountains nearby, and the boys hiked in them carrying packs. Ed had been told that during his stay he would need no more than five dollars, but I soon got a letter. I sent him forty dollars to help him get the things he wanted. This was very different from when I was a boy. My family was poor, and we had so little.

As the boys grew older, they wanted to go into the services. Joe volunteered for the U.S. Navy in April 1956. He was assigned to the Seabees and, after some months of training, came home to be with us at Christmas. Then he was sent to Spain and later to the Caribbean. That same year, Edward graduated from high school. He enlisted in the U.S. Army and took his recruit training. Assigned to the Signal Corps, he studied radio at Fort Monmouth. He also came home to be with us at Christmas, and then he went to Germany. After the boys left again, it was an especially lonely life for my wife.

One day our chief told all the Papagos to come to a meeting in the Rock House, our headquarters across the road from the San Xavier Mission. He said that someone was going to tell us about the Duval Mining Company wanting to prospect and mine for copper on our reservation land. Our people had already heard about this. Those of us who owned land southwest of the San Xavier Mission were asked to lease our land. My two brothers and I agreed to the lease. Later we were told that we had some money waiting for us at the Papago Headquarters in Sells.

For some time I had thought of building a good house. I planned to build east of the Mission, near the house we had lived in since 1950. I bought some bricks and was getting ready to start when Mr. Lyman Priest, the Indian Agency real estate man, told me that the tribe was going to be leasing that land soon. He wanted me to move a quarter of a mile west of the

Mission onto a triple lot. I liked the new place better because it was closer to our people. I had to move all of my bricks in a little trailer which I had.

I started our new home in 1958, and I had a very good helper, my Mrs. She worked very hard, and we worked every day. We drove from our old home, but, when it got cold, sometimes we would work only half a day. I laid out the house, dug the footings, and began to lay the brick. My Mrs. would hand me bricks, passing each one up as I began to build higher. It took us several months before we reached the height we wanted to go.

One morning in November, when I took a bucket of mixed cement up about five feet on the scaffold, I stepped on the edge of the board and down I went. The cement bucket landed on top of me. My head hit the brick wall, and I was knocked unconscious. I do not know how long I lay there. My wife was frozen. She just stood there looking at me. As I woke up, it felt like my head was busted and my hip was broken. I couldn't move. I noticed my Mrs. was standing there just looking at me. I silently prayed some of the words I remembered, and then I got up smiling. I laughed and asked her what had happened. I had concrete all over my clothes and face, but right away I climbed up and went to work laying bricks again.

When the row of bricks was about eight feet high, we were ready to put in the beams, the rafters, and the roof. After that we were ready to work inside. A friend, Mr. Lionel Drake, knew that we had finished the outside and came to help. He knew much about wiring. When we finished I tried to pay him for his work, but he would not accept anything.

Early in 1959 we were still working on the house, but the inside work was coming along fine. One day we went home after working on the new house, and we could see that somebody had broken into our old house through a window. When I unlocked the door, I saw our son Joe lying sound asleep on the bed. We were surprised, but pleased. He had finished his enlistment in the Navy. From his work in the Seabees' construction battalion he had learned much about carpentry, and he could help us. Our older son, Edward, came home from Germany in June, and by that time we were in our new home.

After Joe had helped me finish our new home, he began working on construction jobs around the Tucson area. One of the most interesting jobs was working on the V-shaped telescope building on Kitt Peak. The workers had to drive up a very steep and dangerous trail each day to reach the mountain top. Then he worked on the city-government building and a large bowling building. When the Duval Mining Company began to put up their buildings, he worked on them.

Joe was the first of our boys to start a family. He married a white girl, Miss Terre Kindle, in 1965, and they built a home right next to mine. Joe and his wife had two sons, James II and Joseph, which made my Mrs. very happy. In later years, Joe did not have good health, and he was not able to work regularly. He was very good at making bicycles and other things from used parts, and he sold them to many people.

Edward took a job working at the Mission Mine as a crushing-mill operator, and he held this job for over twenty years. Ed was like his father, in that he did not marry early. He married a white girl, Miss Martha Merkel, and in 1982 they had a baby girl, Kateri. The Mrs. was very happy again.

After I finished that house in 1959, my working days were over. I stayed home and did things around the house. My Mrs. and I planted a good garden each year, and I got to where I liked to watch television programs. I bought a number of books, mostly about other countries, and enjoyed reading them.

Once we had settled in our new home, I had more time to visit and know our people. I was surprised when one day in the 1960s, I was asked to be on the District Council. At that time, our tribal chairman was Enos Francisco, and Harry Throssell, whom I had known as a boy, was also on the District Council. I served three times—I became a veteran councilman.

Tribal and district councilmen were present when they inaugurated the solar telescope at Kitt Peak on November 2, 1962. Kitt Peak is on Papago land, and it was only with our agreement that the National Observatory had been built there. Harry Throssell and I went from San Xavier, and John Manuel came from the Gila Bend District. John was already eighty, and I remembered him from my Phoenix Indian School days in 1916. Albert Martínez was there, and he and I had our picture taken on top of the solar telescope. The inauguration was a big affair, and a government bus took us up Kitt Peak. There were many high officials from different parts of the United States. I remember that Mr. Stewart Udall, Secretary of the Interior, and his wife came. Scientists showed us how the solar telescope worked, and then everybody was served dinner in the big telescope tunnel. More than a hundred people were served at a long table.

In 1975 there was a parade in Sells, our tribal capital, on Veterans Day. I went to watch, and I was wearing my khaki shirt and campaign hat, which I had from the days when I was in the regulars. I had also pinned on my marksmanship medal. Col. Robert Piccola, then commander of a veterans' group called AMVETS, came over and talked to me. I told him that I had been gassed and wounded during World War I. When he asked me why I didn't wear my Purple Heart Medal, I told him that the Army hadn't given me one. The Colonel got very interested and wrote the Army. About four months later, the Army sent the Purple Heart and an Oak Leaf Cluster. I was also awarded a World War I Victory Medal with two campaign bars. I was very proud when on November 13, 1976, AMVETS held a service, read my citation, and Mr. Eugene Allgood, their adjutant, pinned the medal on me. These awards came almost sixty years after the war.

After our sons came back from the service, Edward and I, and sometimes Emilia, took trips to visit the places where I had gone to school and work. The first trip was in 1965, when the three of us went to visit New Mexico and Colorado. In Albuquerque we found the old Indian school. The old buildings were not much changed, but there were some new buildings. When we got to Santa Fe, it was difficult to locate the school. It had been five or six miles out in the country when I was there in 1914, but by the mid-1960s it was surrounded by a highway and the town. There were new buildings, and the old elementary school was now, instead, an Indian school of art. After we left Santa Fe, we went to Rocky Ford and then retraced the long hike which I had made from Colorado to Arizona in 1915.

In 1969, we took another long trip to Oregon and Washington to visit the Klamath reservation. The only man I expected to see, Big Jim, had died the previous year. We came back by way of California and saw many of the places where I had worked and the family had lived. We made another trip to visit Albuquerque and Santa Fe in 1970. We even made one trip to the West Coast to see a professional football bowl game.

In the late 1960s a good nurse used to visit our family, especially to check on the health of Joe's son, baby James II. She was interested in the different desert plants. I told her about them and how many of them we used to use for food. In my young days, I did not eat many things sold in stores. The old people knew what to eat in the desert, where they lived all their lives. Our people, though poor, seemed to have better eyes, be less fat, and to be in better health than today. The nurse, after hearing me tell about my life on the Big Reservation, old Tucson, Indian schools, the Army, Alaska, and California, said to me, "Why don't you write your life story?"

Several times I started, but I left it because I had many things to do. I have done my best, but big words are hard to spell, and I never finished elementary school. I have had much to write about, for life has been good to me in many ways. I have had a good wife, good sons, and I have enough money to live on and, sometimes, to help others. It was hard in my early life. Then my work was heavy and the pay very low. I could not save much, but I met many interesting people and I often think of them. Of course, most are dead now, for many years have gone by.

My family was not as fortunate as I. My father, José Antone, was always poor and died in a car accident in 1920. La-Lee, my mother, lived to be 102; she died in 1954. Mostly she had lived with José Domingo, my oldest brother, who never married. Mother's death was really caused by the marriage of my younger brother Grover to an old Navajo woman. Grover's wife was almost eighty years old—almost twice as old as he was. Why he would marry someone so old and poor and different in language and religion, she couldn't understand. She was bitter . . . it killed her.

Nicolás, my next younger brother, lived on the Big Reservation and had a wife and three daughters. Nick was killed in a truck accident at Rillito. His wife, Chana, later became blind. In the 1980s one daughter lived on the reservation and another in Tucson. The third daughter, Sister Loucia, was a nun in Wisconsin.

Sarah, my sister, married a man I never met. They had one baby, who died very early. Sarah died about 1937. Grover lived with his old Navajo woman till she died some years later. After some more years he died of alcohol. My brother Fernando died in middle age of some disease we never knew. My youngest brother, John, shot himself one day in December 1937. He was at my aunt's place, back of the Rock House, which was then our district headquarters. The Yaqui Festival was underway, and, just as the fireworks began, he took his life. We don't know why.

I have been in fairly good health ever since Mr. Gunnersen taught me about the science of life. I still have my books on eschatology by Mr. Walter, and the little black books in which I wrote my prayers. I haven't healed anybody since I left my job at the Hotel Geronimo. You can only heal people if they have faith, and today the Papagos don't believe in anything, so I can't help them.

I didn't go to doctors until October 1983, when I had a heart attack. I fell down in my yard; I couldn't talk, and I vomited. Joe took me to the Indian Health Clinic at San Xavier, and they sent me to the clinic at Sells. Neither helped me. I was weak, and I lost weight. I went to a medicine man, but he didn't make me well. After a time I went to the Veterans Hospital in Tucson. I had a woman doctor, and she put me in bed for two or three weeks. X-rays showed something cloudy in my lungs, and a doctor wanted to operate, but I wouldn't agree to it. Soon the doctors said that the cloud had cleared up.

After this the doctors wanted to do a little operation. I didn't understand quite what it was, but I agreed. They installed a pacemaker to make my heart work better. When I left the hospital, the doctors told me to take it easy and not to chop wood anymore. In spite of that, I won a blanket for dancing in all of the dances at the Papago Festival at San Xavier in March of 1984.

A few months before, in December 1983, my Mrs. fell ill, and we had a doctor come see her several times. She went to Sells for treatment and then to St. Mary's Hospital in Tucson. She did not get better, and, on January 12, 1984, she died. My Mrs. was a good woman—quiet and a hard worker. For awhile I didn't want to live in the home that we had built together. I lived for some months with my son Edward and his family. They were nice to me, but I missed the quiet of my home. It's lonesome, but the children and grandchildren visit often—and I have my memories.

Sometimes when I'm alone, I feel a tug at my arm, as if someone were pulling me. There's no one there. I talked with the medicine men about this, and they tell me that the unseen visitors are my ancestors, family, and friends. They are calling me to join them. When I do, we'll be a complete family again, for I am the last of my generation.

Index

Ajo, 10, 70, 118; fire in, 155 – 156;
McCarthy's police work in,
156 – 158; shop work in,
153 – 154; work in mines at,
115 – 117

Alaska, 121 – 128

Alberto (Mexican laborer in
Hemet), 172, 173 – 174

Albuquerque, New Mexico, 55, 63

Albuquerque Indian School,
49 – 51, 55, 63 – 64

American Red Cross, 85, 87

AMVETS, 190

Antone, Fernando (brother), 26,
192

Antone, Grover (brother), 103,
119, 192

Antone, John (brother), 105, 115,
145, 192

Antone, José (father), 1, 72, 82;
death of, 92, 192; family life of,
7, 8, 22, 23, 27; moves to

Chandler, 62; moves to Tucson,
5, 6; ranch of, 108

Antone, José and Ceba (great-
uncle and great-aunt), 152

Antone, José Domingo (brother),
72, 105, 145, 151; car accident of,
92; death of, 192; helps McCarthy clear farm, 148; and Indian
schools, 5, 47 – 48; moves to
Coolidge, 147; protects younger
brothers, 37

Antone, La-Lee (mother), 14; and
McCarthy's early life, 1 – 2, 7,
9, 23, 24, 26 – 27; and McCarthy's mining injuries, 116 – 117;
and McCarthy's return from
Phoenix Indian School, 35; in
car accident, 92; death of, 192;
early life of, 13; encourages
McCarthy and Emilia, 147; as
family banker, 107; work of, 7,
8, 22, 26, 105

All entries for James McCarthy are listed under "McCarthy, James," regardless of the name he may have used at the time of the event. Parents of James
McCarthy and their other children are listed under the "Antone" surname, regardless of the names they have used. All place names indexed are Arizona
unless otherwise stated.

Index

Antone, Nicolás (brother), 111;
  birth of, 5; death of, 192; and
  father's ranch, 108; family of,
  105; and Hugh Norris, 26; at
  Sante Fe Indian School, 38 – 39,
  42, 45, 49, 51
Antone, Sarah (sister), 26, 105,
  115, 145, 192
Apaches, 9, 111
Archky, Mr. (director of school
  work camps), 43, 46, 51

Banning Homes, 164
Baseball, 40 – 41, 49 – 51, 51 – 52,
  64, 97, 100 – 101, 127, 149 – 150
Benito (uncle), 5
Be-tas-coo-a-wa-tam (Acting
  Like Sun), 17 – 18
Bethlehem Steel Corporation, 171
Big Field Village, 109, 112
Big Jim, 133 – 136
Bisbee, 70, 71
Blackwater, 113, 151
Blaine, Joe, 158
Brawley, California, 143, 145
Brown, J. B., 64, 65, 68
Buffington, Webster, 68, 69, 74, 78,
  83
Burbank, California, 120

Cababi, 11 – 13, 21, 107
Cabrillo Park (Tucson), 22 – 23
Calexico, California, 145, 173
Cally (Circle Going), 1
Camp Dix, New Jersey, 74 – 75, 87,
  88
Camp Kearney, California, 72 – 74
Carline, Mrs. (faith healer), 154
Car-me (cousin), 9 – 22, 107, 113
Casa Grande, 33, 107, 108, 114, 151
Chew-Lo-Moon, 15, 18, 19
China, 90 – 96
Christian Science Church, 171,
  178, 180
Circle Walk, 13, 108
Clovis, California, 140, 141
Columbia River, 134 – 138
Comobabi Village, 8, 11, 21, 62
Con-nee-Law, 113 – 114
Consolidated Steel Corporation,
  163, 171
Coolidge, 116, 147
Covered Wells, 13, 108

Crandall, Clinton, 41, 43, 48 – 51
Cuate (Lorenzo McCormick),
  6 – 7

Drake, Lionel, 187
Drinking, 155 – 157
Drugs, 102 – 103, 122, 124, 125,
  126
Duval Mining Company, 186, 188

El Centro, California, 120,
  142 – 145
England, 76 – 77
Escondido, California, 138, 154
Eskimos, 121, 126, 127
Estrella, Manuel, 150 – 151
Eugeno (Navajo loafer), 129 – 132

Faith healing, 165 – 170, 173 – 174,
  176 – 177, 178, 180 – 183, 193
Farming, 148 – 149, 151, 152 – 153
Federal Bureau of Investigation
  (F.B.I.), 63, 124 – 125, 156 – 157
Fernando (boy in San Luis), 112
Fishing, 134 – 136
Fiston, Miss (teacher), 56, 67
Flagstaff, 56, 65
Florence, 113, 119
Foot, José, 105, 110
France, 77 – 85, 87
Francisco, Enos, 189
Francisco, Nestro, 119
Francisco, Patriso, 30 – 33, 35,
  40 – 41, 47
Fresno, California, 117, 118, 140

Gambling, 19, 21, 91, 99 – 100, 109
Germany, prison camp in, 85 – 87
Geronimo Hotel (Tucson),
  179 – 184
Gila River Pima Reservation, 31,
  113, 147, 151 – 153
Gilmore, Guy, 49
Girllee, Mr. ("Cowskin"; disci-
  plinarian, Santa Fe Indian
  School), 41, 45, 49, 50
Goodyear Company Farms,
  105 – 107, 108, 146
Goodyear Rubber plant, 161
Grestead, Major (disciplinarian,
  Phoenix Indian School), 29, 66
Gunnerson, Harry, 164 – 169, 178,
  193

Ha-sa-kit (In Middle), 17
Hemet, California, 171 – 174
Hoboken, New Jersey, 87
Honolulu, Hawaii, 88, 97
Hubbard, Captain William J. H. (mine foreman), 117

Imperial Valley, California, 142, 145
Indians. *See* Apaches; Navajos; Nez Percé; Papagos; Pimas; Toppenish; Yakimas; Yaquis; Zunis
Indians, attitudes of people toward, 74 – 75, 76 – 77, 86, 95, 163
Indians in movies, 121, 138 – 139
Indian schools: clothing at, 28; curriculum at, 29, 40 – 42, 48, 49, 66 – 67; discipline at, 28 – 30, 49, 66 – 67; food at, 41 – 42; forgetting families at, 42, 43, 45; McCarthy's reception at, 28, 40; running away from, 29 – 35, 53 – 59; sports and recreation at, 40 – 41, 47, 49 – 51, 61, 64; summer activities of, 43 – 47, 51 – 53, 61 – 62; travel to, 27 – 28, 38 – 39, 61 – 64, 65 – 66
Indian volunteers in World War I, 68
Iron Stand, 1, 9, 13, 19, 111
Isleta Indian Village, New Mexico, 55

Japan, 89 – 90
Japanese-American family, relationship of, with McCarthy, 46 – 47, 51
John (Toppenish Indian Reservation policeman), 131 – 133
Jolley, Jim, 176, 177
Juan (uncle, called Jack Rabbit), 7
Juanita (niece of Charlie Jobe), 133, 135 – 137

Kickball (We-ch), 8 – 9, 18 – 21
Kidnapping of Indian boy, 23 – 24
Kitt Peak National Observatory, 188, 189 – 190
Klamath Indian Reservation, 191
Kuyriles, Mrs. (Sunday school superintendent), 178

Lamy Junction, New Mexico, 39, 44, 46, 47, 55
Lawrence, Susie (niece), 147
Liberty, 105
Litchfield Park, 104, 106, 109, 113, 115, 118, 145, 178
Littlefield, 1, 13, 18, 21, 107
Lockwood, Hudson, 74, 78
Long Beach, California, 159, 175
Longry Aircraft Company, 163
Los Angeles, California, 120, 138 – 139, 171, 177
Louis, John, 148, 153
Lowell, 70 – 71
Luime Park Trailer Court, 160, 164

McCarthy, Edward (son), 157; birth and baptism of, 152; marriage and family of, 188 – 189; military service of, 186, 188; offers a home to his father, 194; in school, 178; scouting activities of, 185 – 186; and trips with McCarthy, 190 – 191
McCarthy, Emilia (née Castillo; wife): and birth of children, 152, 169; and building of retirement home, 187 – 188; death of, 193 – 194; and eschatology, 169; nurses McCarthy, 161 – 162
McCarthy, James: in Alaska, 121 – 128; Army discharges of, 87, 98; and baseball, 40 – 41, 49 – 52, 97, 100 – 101; birth of, 1; at Camp Dix, 74 – 75; at Camp Kearney, 72 – 74; in China, 90 – 96; in Colorado, 43 – 47, 51 – 53; and the death of Emilia, 193 – 194; and the Depression, 140 – 145, 151 – 152; in England, 76 – 77; and faith healing, 164 – 177, 180 – 183, 193; heart attack of, 193; at Indian school in Albuquerque, 64 – 65; at Indian school in Phoenix, 26 – 38, 61, 64 – 67; at Indian school in Santa Fe, 38 – 53; at Indian schools in Tucson, 5, 36; injuries and hospitalizations of, 73, 81 – 83, 84 – 85, 87, 92, 116 – 117, 150, 161 – 162, 164 – 170, 187, 193; in Japan, 89 – 90; and the

McCarthy, James *(continued)*
kickball race, 18 – 21; and
miners' strike, 70 – 71; names
of, 2, 56, 60, 69; National
Guard service of, 68 – 72; and
Papago festivals, 14 – 18,
109 – 110, 111; in the Philippines, 89, 93 – 94, 96 – 97;
reenlistment of, 87; reflections
of, about the future, 194; remi-
nisces about family, 191 – 192;
retirement home of, 186 – 188;
retirement trips of, 190 – 191;
travels of, by foot, 30 – 35,
53 – 57; travels of, by ship,
75 – 76, 77, 87, 88 – 90, 97,
122 – 124, 128; travels of, by
train, 27 – 28, 39, 43, 44, 46, 47,
57 – 59, 62 – 64, 65, 72, 74,
77 – 78, 104; and Toppenish
Indians, 130 – 133, 134, 136;
trips of, to Big Reservation,
9 – 22, 107 – 112; works at cannery, 121 – 128; works as
boilerman, 125 – 128; works
as farmer, 43 – 47, 51 – 53,
117 – 118, 139 – 145, 148 – 153;
works at Goodyear Farms,
104 – 107; works as hotel maintenance man, 179 – 184; works
as industrial worker, 161 – 164,
171; works as migrant worker,
100 – 104, 117 – 118, 140 – 145,
171 – 172, 174; works as miner,
115 – 117; works in mine shops,
153 – 154; works at Montezuma
Sanitarium, 59 – 62; works as
movie extra, 121; works as
muleskinner, 118 – 120; works
in Navy shipyard, 175 – 178;
works for packing company,
129; works as policeman,
156 – 158; works for railroad,
53, 103, and World War I, 68,
74 – 87, 190

McCarthy, James II (grandson),
188, 191
McCarthy, Joseph (son): birth of,
157; marriage of, 188; military
service of, 186, 188; schooling
of, 178, 185
McCarthy, Joseph (grandson), 188

McCarthy, Martha (née Merkel;
daughter-in-law), 189
McCarthy, Terre (née Kindle;
daughter-in-law), 188
McCormick, Lorenzo (Cuate), 6,
7
Ma-e-tan, Jim (Car-me's hus-
band, 9 – 10, 13, 18, 153
Magdalena, Sonora, 1, 118
Manuel, John, 189
Manzanola, Colorado, 43
María (captured Papago girl), 9
María, José (uncle), 5
María, Juan, 59 – 62
Maricopa, 32, 33
Martindale, Rose Pardner, 169
Martínez, Albert, 189
Mary (Big Jim's wife), 135
Matthew, Miss, cured by
McCarthy, 181 – 183
Mexican Revolution, 69
Miami, 70, 119
Miguel, Hilare, 139 – 144
Miners' strike, 69 – 71
Mining, 115 – 117
Mission mine, 188
Molino, Elmer (cousin), 160, 161
Mo-M-La-Lee (called Sharp
Money), 15, 17, 20
Montezuma Sanitarium,
Phoenix, 59 – 62
Morris brothers, Elias and
Harvey, 106
Muleskinning, 118 – 120

Naco, 69 – 72, 80
National Guard of Arizona,
McCarthy's service in, 68 – 72
Navajos, 50
New York, New York, 74 – 75
Nez Percé, 133
Nogales, 6, 118
Norris, Hugh, 5, 26 – 27, 38
Norton, Jack, 132
Now-a-Chew, 15, 16

Ocheo, Ciprano, 156, 157
Ortega, Juan and Mary, 159

Pan Tak, 1, 11
Papagos (Tohono O'Odham,
"Desert People"), 29, 147;
crops of, 2, 12 – 14, 17, 23, 24,

148; and drinking, 111, 155 – 157; and faith healing, 193; festivals and ceremonies of, 15 – 18, 109 – 110, 113, 193; food preparation by, 11, 18 – 19, 36 – 37, 44, 151; gambling by, 19 – 21; legends of, 17, 114; marriage customs of, 147; reservations of, 1, 9, 36, 39, 107; and sports, 8 – 9, 19 – 21
Pascola, 15, 114
Pennington family, 179 – 181, 184
Perce, Mr. (Superintendent, Albuquerque Indian School), 51, 64, 65
Perschl, Father Nicholas, 159
Philippines, the, 89, 93 – 94, 96 – 97
Phoenix, 26, 57, 58, 62, 65, 88, 104 – 105, 107, 119, 139, 142, 149
Phoenix Indian School, 27 – 30, 61, 64 – 67; running away from, 29 – 35
Piccola, Colonel Robert, 190
Pimas (River People), 29, 32, 104, 149; reservations of, 31, 113, 116, 148 – 149, 151 – 153
Portland, Oregon, 130, 137 – 138
Prescott, 57, 58
Presidio, San Francisco, California, 88, 98
Prison camp in Germany, 85 – 87
Pueblo, Colorado, 53 – 54
Purple Heart decoration, 190

Queen, José, 113 – 115
Queen, Mrs. José (cousin), 105

Railroads: Santa Fe, 103; Southern Pacific, 27, 32 – 35, 38 – 39, 62 – 63
Rain-making ceremony, 109 – 110
Rincon Mountains, 23, 24
Riverbank, California, 103, 104
Rocky Ford, Colorado, 43, 46, 47, 52, 53, 65, 191

Sacaton, 105, 113, 150, 152
Sacramento, California, 99 – 101
St. Mary's Hospital, Tucson, 92, 193
Salt River, 31

San Carlos Village and Dam, 118 – 119
San Francisco, California, 37, 88, 98, 122, 128, 129
San José (story teller), 114
San Louis, 108
San Luis, 108, 111 – 112
San Pedro, California, 159, 164, 171, 174
Santa Cruz River, 2, 4, 37
Santa Fe Indian School, 37 – 55, 190 – 191
Santa Rosa, 1, 13, 108, 113
San Xavier Mission, 2, 152, 158 – 159; school of, 5, 26, 48
San Xavier Reservation 1, 11, 39, 82 – 83, 88, 158, 178, 193
Schools. *See* Indian schools
Schuck, Mrs. (Superintendent, Sunnyside School District), 178
Seattle, Washington, 137
Sells (Indian Oasis), 107, 111, 112, 141, 186, 190, 193
Sharp Hat, 114
Sharp Money, 15, 17, 20
Ships, 75 – 76, 77, 87, 88 – 90, 97, 122 – 123, 128
Smith, Chico and Lora, 149, 152
Sonoita, Mexico, 147, 151
Sonora (Papago loafer), 141
Spokane, Washington, 131
Spud (Chinese mascot), 94 – 96
Steven (called Part Yellow; cousin), 109
Stockton, California, 101 – 103
Sweet Mouth (uncle), 109 – 111

Talafa, Nero, 40, 55, 64
Throssell, Henry (Harry), 36, 189
Throssell, Thomas, 36
Todd Shipyard, 171
Toppenish, 130, 131, 132 – 134, 136
Torrance, California, 160, 163
Trains. *See* McCarthy, James, travels of, by train; Railroads
Trinidad, Colorado, 47
Tucson, 62 – 63, 72, 112, 118, 148, 178; Indian schools in, 37, 48; McCarthy's early life in, 5, 6 – 8, 10, 22 – 23; McCarthy returns permanently to, 178, 185

Index

Udall, Stewart, 189
United States Army: awards
  McCarthy the Purple Heart,
  190; in China, 90 – 93, 94 – 96;
  garrison life in, 90 – 97;
  McCarthy's combat in, during
  World War I, 78 – 84; McCarthy's discharges from, 87, 98;
  McCarthy's peacetime service
  in, 88 – 98; McCarthy's
  reenlistment in, 87; and
  machine gun drill team,
  93 – 94; in the Philippines,
  93 – 94, 96 – 97; and transport
  of McCarthy's unit to Europe,
  75 – 78. See also National
  Guard of Arizona; Camp Dix;
  Camp Kearney
United States Navy Shipyard,
  Long Beach, California,
  175 – 178

Val-Leea (cousin), 109
Vane, Mr. (coach, Phoenix Indian
  School), 65 – 66

Vekol, 12, 16, 18
Veterans Administration, 151, 193

Walm, Mineral, 172 – 174
Walter, William, 166 – 167, 170,
  180, 182 – 183, 193
We-ch (kickball), 8 – 9, 18 – 21
Wellton, 119
Wentz Brothers Packing Com-
  pany, 36
West, Mrs. (Sunday school
  teacher), 174
White, Mrs. (owner, Montezuma
  Sanitarium), 60 – 62
Wobblies, 70 – 71
Woodruff, Mrs. Janette, 2, 72,
  82 – 83, 92
World War I, 67, 68, 74 – 87

Yakimas, 133, 146
Yaquis, 15, 105, 192
Yuma, 104, 117

Zunis, 101 – 103